LGBTQIA+ Rights

Other Books of Related Interest

Opposing Viewpoints Series
Gender in the 21st Century
Marriage
Reproductive Rights

At Issue Series
Male Privilege
Sexual Consent
Universal Health Care

Current Controversies Series
America's Mental Health Crisis
Domestic Extremism
Hate Groups

> "Congress shall make no law ... abridging the freedom of speech, or of the press."
>
> *First Amendment to the U.S. Constitution*

The basic foundation of our democracy is the First Amendment guarantee of freedom of expression. The Opposing Viewpoints series is dedicated to the concept of this basic freedom and the idea that it is more important to practice it than to enshrine it.

LGBTQIA+ Rights

Avery Elizabeth Hurt, Book Editor

Published in 2023 by Greenhaven Publishing, LLC
2544 Clinton Street,
Buffalo NY 14224

Copyright © 2023 by Greenhaven Publishing, LLC

First Edition

All rights reserved. No part of this book may be reproduced in any form
without permission in writing from the publisher, except by a reviewer.

Articles in Greenhaven Publishing anthologies are often edited for length to meet page
requirements. In addition, original titles of these works are changed to clearly present
the main thesis and to explicitly indicate the author's opinion. Every effort is made to
ensure that Greenhaven Publishing accurately reflects the original intent of the authors.
Every effort has been made to trace the owners of the copyrighted material.

Cover image: Angyalosi Beata/Shutterstock.com.

Library of Congress CataloginginPublication Data

Names: Hurt, Avery Elizabeth, editor.
Title: LGBTQIA+ rights / Avery Elizabeth Hurt, book editor.
Description: First edition. | New York : Greenhaven Publishing, 2023. |
  Series: Opposing viewpoints | Includes bibliographical references and
  index.
Identifiers: LCCN 2022055603 | ISBN 9781534509306 (library binding) | ISBN
  9781534509290 (paperback)
Subjects: LCSH: Gay rights--United States. | Sexual minorities--Civil
  rights--United States.
Classification: LCC HQ76.8.U5 L46 2023 | DDC
  306.76/60973--dc23/eng/20221122
LC record available at https://lccn.loc.gov/2022055603

Manufactured in the United States of America

Website: http://greenhavenpublishing.com

Contents

| The Importance of Opposing Viewpoints | 11 |
| Introduction | 14 |

Chapter 1: What Is the Current State of LGBTQIA+ Rights?

Chapter Preface	18
1. States Pass a Slew of Anti-LGBTQIA+ Legislation *Wyatt Ronan*	19
2. LGBTQIA+ Acceptance Differs Among Nations *Jacob Poushter and Nicholas Kent*	25
3. U.S. Voters Are Increasingly Willing to Elect LGBTQIA+ Candidates *Los Angeles Blade*	33
4. High Court Ruling Does Not Bode Well for LGBTQIA+ Rights *Morgan Marietta*	39
5. Protection of LGBTQIA+ Rights Has an Uneven History *Paul J. Angelo and Dominic Bocci*	45
6. Acceptance of Same-Sex Marriage Has Increased Over Time *Tim Lindberg*	53
Periodical and Internet Sources Bibliography	59

Chapter 2: How Do Transgender Rights Affect Participation in Sports?

Chapter Preface	62
1. It's Harmful to Ban Trans People from Sports *Wren Sanders*	63
2. The NCAA Should Change Its Regulations Regarding Trans Athletes *Evan Mills*	70

3. Transgender Women Should Compete, but Only If They've Mitigated the Advantages of Male Puberty   74
   Nancy Hogshead-Makar
4. We Need Better Solutions for Gender-Segregated Sports   83
   Katharina Lindner
5. A Balance Must Be Struck Between Fairness in Sports and Transgender Rights   87
   Chris W. Surprenant

Periodical and Internet Sources Bibliography   94

Chapter 3: How Do LGBTQIA+ Rights Affect Health Care and Safety?

Chapter Preface   97

1. LGBTQIA+ People Still Face Discrimination in Health Care   98
   Jessica N. Fish
2. Disparities Exist in Mental Health Care for LGBTQIA+ People   103
   Willem Stander
3. The Ethics of Who Should Provide Gender-Affirming Care Are Complex   107
   Cary S. Crall and Rachel K. Jackson
4. LGBTQIA+ Youth Face Higher Risk of Suicide   114
   The Trevor Project
5. Compassionate Care Is Needed to Address Health Inequality in LGBTQIA+ Communities   125
   Phillip Joy, Andrew Thomas, and Megan Aston
6. LGBTQIA+ People Face a Heightened Risk of Hate Crimes   130
   Andrew Ryan Flores, Ilan Meyer, and Rebecca Stotzer

Periodical and Internet Sources Bibliography   134

Chapter 4: Should Transgender People Be Allowed to Serve in the Military?

Chapter Preface	137
1. Bias Remains a Problem for LGBTQIA+ Service Members *Meghann Myers*	138
2. There Are Gender-Related Differences in Opinions on Gender-Neutral Bathrooms in the Military *Mike Krings*	144
3. Transgender Service Members Will Weaken the Military *Thomas Spoehr*	149
4. Transgender Service Members Will Make the Military Stronger *Christian Fuscarino*	153
5. Transgender Troops Are Fit to Serve in the Military *Brandon Hill and Joshua Trey Barnett*	157
Periodical and Internet Sources Bibliography	**162**
For Further Discussion	164
Organizations to Contact	167
Bibliography of Books	171
Index	173

The Importance of Opposing Viewpoints

Perhaps every generation experiences a period in time in which the populace seems especially polarized, starkly divided on the important issues of the day and gravitating toward the far ends of the political spectrum and away from a consensus-facilitating middle ground. The world that today's students are growing up in and that they will soon enter into as active and engaged citizens is deeply fragmented in just this way. Issues relating to terrorism, immigration, women's rights, minority rights, race relations, health care, taxation, wealth and poverty, the environment, policing, military intervention, the proper role of government—in some ways, perennial issues that are freshly and uniquely urgent and vital with each new generation—are currently roiling the world.

If we are to foster a knowledgeable, responsible, active, and engaged citizenry among today's youth, we must provide them with the intellectual, interpretive, and critical-thinking tools and experience necessary to make sense of the world around them and of the all-important debates and arguments that inform it. After all, the outcome of these debates will in large measure determine the future course, prospects, and outcomes of the world and its peoples, particularly its youth. If they are to become successful members of society and productive and informed citizens, students need to learn how to evaluate the strengths and weaknesses of someone else's arguments, how to sift fact from opinion and fallacy, and how to test the relative merits and validity of their own opinions against the known facts and the best possible available information. The landmark series Opposing Viewpoints has been providing students with just such critical-thinking skills and exposure to the debates surrounding society's most urgent contemporary issues for many years, and it continues to serve this essential role with undiminished commitment, care, and rigor.

The key to the series's success in achieving its goal of sharpening students' critical-thinking and analytic skills resides in its title—

Opposing Viewpoints. In every intriguing, compelling, and engaging volume of this series, readers are presented with the widest possible spectrum of distinct viewpoints, expert opinions, and informed argumentation and commentary, supplied by some of today's leading academics, thinkers, analysts, politicians, policy makers, economists, activists, change agents, and advocates. Every opinion and argument anthologized here is presented objectively and accorded respect. There is no editorializing in any introductory text or in the arrangement and order of the pieces. No piece is included as a "straw man," an easy ideological target for cheap point-scoring. As wide and inclusive a range of viewpoints as possible is offered, with no privileging of one particular political ideology or cultural perspective over another. It is left to each individual reader to evaluate the relative merits of each argument—as he or she sees it, and with the use of ever-growing critical-thinking skills—and grapple with his or her own assumptions, beliefs, and perspectives to determine how convincing or successful any given argument is and how the reader's own stance on the issue may be modified or altered in response to it.

This process is facilitated and supported by volume, chapter, and selection introductions that provide readers with the essential context they need to begin engaging with the spotlighted issues, with the debates surrounding them, and with their own perhaps shifting or nascent opinions on them. In addition, guided reading and discussion questions encourage readers to determine the authors' point of view and purpose, interrogate and analyze the various arguments and their rhetoric and structure, evaluate the arguments' strengths and weaknesses, test their claims against available facts and evidence, judge the validity of the reasoning, and bring into clearer, sharper focus the reader's own beliefs and conclusions and how they may differ from or align with those in the collection or those of their classmates.

Research has shown that reading comprehension skills improve dramatically when students are provided with compelling, intriguing, and relevant "discussable" texts. The subject matter of

The Importance of Opposing Viewpoints

these collections could not be more compelling, intriguing, or urgently relevant to today's students and the world they are poised to inherit. The anthologized articles and the reading and discussion questions that are included with them also provide the basis for stimulating, lively, and passionate classroom debates. Students who are compelled to anticipate objections to their own argument and identify the flaws in those of an opponent read more carefully, think more critically, and steep themselves in relevant context, facts, and information more thoroughly. In short, using discussable text of the kind provided by every single volume in the Opposing Viewpoints series encourages close reading, facilitates reading comprehension, fosters research, strengthens critical thinking, and greatly enlivens and energizes classroom discussion and participation. The entire learning process is deepened, extended, and strengthened.

For all of these reasons, Opposing Viewpoints continues to be exactly the right resource at exactly the right time—when we most need to provide readers with the critical-thinking tools and skills that will not only serve them well in school but also in their careers and their daily lives as decision-making family members, community members, and citizens. This series encourages respectful engagement with and analysis of opposing viewpoints and fosters a resulting increase in the strength and rigor of one's own opinions and stances. As such, it helps make readers "future ready," and that readiness will pay rich dividends for the readers themselves, for the citizenry, for our society, and for the world at large.

Introduction

> "Equality means more than passing laws. The struggle is really won in the hearts and minds of the community, where it really counts."
>
> – Barbara Gittings, American LGBTQIA+ activist

First, let's get some terminology straight. LGBTQIA+—that's a lot of letters. Here's what they stand for:

- L is for lesbian
- G is for gay
- B is for bisexual
- T is for transgender
- Q is for queer or questioning
- I is for intersex
- A is for asexual
- And the plus sign is for gender identities that don't fit into any of the above categories.

When you put them all together, you get . . . a lot of people. There are many gender identities, and that long string of letters is an attempt to include them all. There are other ways to refer to this community—some with more letters, some with less—but in this volume, we've chosen to use LGBTQIA+ because it's pretty inclusive. More than just having a letter for every gender identity (which would probably be impossible to do), here the term LGBTQIA+ is meant, as much as anything else, as a reminder that there are many ways people define their genders, and that no matter how they define it, they all want to be included. This book is about that fight for inclusion.

Many people mark the beginning of the LGBTQIA+ rights movement with the Stonewall uprising. One June night in 1969, police raided the Stonewall Inn in New York City. At the time, homosexuality was illegal in New York (even cross-dressing was illegal), and this was not the first time police had raided this popular LGBTQIA+ bar. But this time something snapped. The police got rough, and Stonewall's patrons fought back. The crowd threw things at the police, and the police ended up barricading themselves in the inn. Fortunately, no one was seriously injured. But the event galvanized and united the LGBTQIA+ community. People began peacefully demanding the protection of LGBTQIA+ rights. The first Pride March was held one year later in 1970, on the anniversary of Stonewall.

Since then, LGBTQIA+ people have made a great deal of progress in ensuring their rights. In 2011, the United States Department of Defense repealed its "Don't Ask, Don't Tell," policy which prevented gay and lesbian people from serving openly in the military. In 2015, the Supreme Court ruled, in a case known as *Obergefell v. Hodges*, that same-sex marriage was protected by the U.S. Constitution. In 2021, transgender people were granted the right to serve in the U.S. armed forces.

But it hasn't all been victories for the LGBTQIA+ community. Recently, many states have passed legislation denying the rights of LGBTQIA+ people, especially transgender youth. The LGBTQIA+ rights movement seems to many to be losing ground after decades of advancement. The cultural situation and government policy about LGBTQIA+ people often seems to be ever-changing. The situation is different in different states, and it's different under different presidential administrations. In fact, you might say that culture is transitioning to an acceptance of LGBTQIA+ people and a respect for their rights. In this volume, the authors look at that transition in policy and attitudes and report on its current status.

In Chapter 1, the focus is on the question "What Is the Current State of LGBTQIA+ Rights?" The authors look at both gains and losses for LGBTQIA+ rights in recent years and current attitudes toward LGBTQIA+ rights.

Chapter 2 focuses on transgender people in sports. Do transgender girls and women have an unfair advantage over cisgender girls and women? The answer is not clear, and the voices here look at the many complexities of this questions. The viewpoints in this chapter also consider the delicate balance between protecting the rights of transgender people and maintaining fairness in athletic events.

In Chapter 3, the viewpoints address situations in which policies can put LGBTQIA+ lives at risk. The chapter looks mostly at health care, but also considers how hate crimes and hate crime legislation impact the LGBTQIA+ community.

Chapter 4 takes on the question of transgender people in the military. Some viewpoint authors argue that including transgender service members strengthen America's armed forces; others argue that transgender troops have a detrimental effect. Others discuss the difficulties faced by LGBTQIA+ people in the military, even when they are officially allowed to serve.

Opposing Viewpoints: LGBTQIA+ Rights endeavors to examine the ways in which the fight to protect the rights of LGBTQIA+ people and to ensure the security of additional rights shapes many aspects of society, including policymaking, health care, the military, sports, and the education system. Through including a wide range of viewpoints on the topic, readers will have the opportunity to gain a nuanced understanding of this complex issue.

CHAPTER 1

What Is the Current State of LGBTQIA+ Rights?

Chapter Preface

Not that long ago, the protection of LGBTQIA+ rights seemed a given in the United States, and even though there was still a long way to go, the future looked bright for LGBTQIA+ Americans. When the U.S. Supreme Court ruled in *Obergefell v. Hodges* that same sex couples had the right to marry, and soon after the right of LGBTQIA+ people to serve in the military was affirmed, it seemed to many that the days of LGBTQIA+ discrimination would soon be a thing of the past. It seemed only a matter of time before all the rights of all LGBTQIA+ people were respected and protected.

That joy did not last long, however. Since then, the United States, which has at times seemed a standard-bearer on this issue, in recent years there have been multiple challenges to LGBTQIA+ rights. These challenges include policies set in place during the Trump administration that rolled back protections against discrimination for LGBTQIA+ people in the workplace and elsewhere, foreign policy that de-emphasized support for LGBTQIA+ rights worldwide, and Supreme Court opinions and rulings supporting religious rights over LGBTQIA+ rights when the two conflict.

The authors of the viewpoints in this chapter look at many of the issues and situations surrounding the rapidly changing landscape of LGBTQIA+ rights in American and elsewhere. The chapter opens with a viewpoint that surveys LGBTQIA+ legislation at the state level—and declares 2021 as the worst year in recent history for LGBTQIA+ rights (so far). The next few viewpoints examine public attitudes about LGBTQIA+ rights at home and abroad, LGBTQIA+ representation in the U.S. Congress, and two Supreme Court rulings and accompanying opinions that do not augur well for the rights of the LGBTQIA+ community. The chapter also contains a viewpoint that details how the United States has, at different times, both led the way in defending LGBTQIA+ rights and stumbled backwards when it comes to those protections.

VIEWPOINT 1

> *"These bills are not only harmful and discriminatory, but also represent a failure in our democracy and the commitment elected officials make to protect and serve their constituents."*

States Pass a Slew of Anti-LGBTQIA+ Legislation

Wyatt Ronan

LGBTQIA+ Americans have faced some unexpected setbacks in recent years. In this viewpoint, published in May of 2021, Wyatt Ronan declares that 2021 surpassed 2015 (when 15 anti-LGBTQIA+ bills were signed into law) as the worst year for anti-LGBTQIA+ legislation in recent memory. The viewpoint categorizes the different types of anti-LGBTQIA+ legislation that was passed in 2021 in addition to bills that had been introduced but had not passed at the time of publication. Ronan explains the various ways in which this legislation negatively impacts the rights of LGBTQIA+ people. At the time this viewpoint was published, Wyatt Ronan was senior press secretary for Human Rights Campaign.

"2021 Officially Becomes Worst Year in Recent History for LGBTQ State Legislative Attacks as Unprecedented Number of States Enact Record-Shattering Number of Anti-LGBTQ Measures Into Law," by Wyatt Ronan, Human Rights Campaign, May 7, 2021. Reprinted by permission. Copyright ♥ Human Rights Campaign, Inc. All Rights Reserved. Reproduced with permission. Any further use without the express written consent of the Human Rights Campaign is prohibited.

LGBTQIA+ Rights

As you read, consider the following questions:

1. According to Ronan, what is the motivation for much of this anti-LGBTQIA+ legislation?
2. How do most Americans feel about these laws, according to this viewpoint?
3. In what ways do these types of laws harm the states that enact them?

With an unprecedented number of anti-LGBTQ measures sweeping through state legislatures across the country, 2021 has officially surpassed 2015 as the worst year for anti-LGBTQ legislation in recent history, according to updated tracking and analysis by the Human Rights Campaign (detailed breakdown below). The previous record—set six years ago in 2015, when 15 anti-LGBTQ bills were enacted into law—was broken on Friday, as the seventeenth anti-LGBTQ bill was enacted into law. In addition, 11 anti-LGBTQ bills are on governors' desks awaiting signature or veto and several more are continuing to move through state legislatures across the country.

> The rights of LGBTQ people—and especially transgender people—across the country are being systematically threatened and undermined by national anti-LGBTQ groups coordinating with anti-equality lawmakers to wage an unprecedented war on the LGBTQ community. In fact, some of these bills are similar to or even worse than anti-LGBTQ legislation that has been rejected in previous years, including the Indiana religious refusal bill of 2015 and North Carolina's infamous HB2. Bills that have become law so far this year range from making it a felony to provide transgender youth with life saving health care to banning transgender girls from participating in sports to erasing LGBTQ people from school curriculum to granting broad licenses to discriminate against LGBTQ people. This crisis cannot be ignored and necessitates concrete action from all those with the ability to speak out. These bills are not only harmful and discriminatory, but also represent a failure in our

democracy and the commitment elected officials make to protect and serve their constituents. Now is not the time for reluctance or passivity, it is time to take urgent action to protect the basic rights and humanity of LGBTQ people in America.

—Alphonso David, Human Rights Campaign President

The wave of anti-LGBTQ legislation—a coordinated push led by national anti-LGBTQ groups, not local lawmakers—is part of a broader strategy to score political points with the conservative base by curtailing the rights of LGBTQ people and specifically trans youth—under the guise of responding to nonexistent and baseless threats. These bills represent a cruel effort to further stigmatize and discriminate against LGBTQ people across the country, specifically trans youth who simply want to live as their true selves and grow into who they are.

Breakdown of Anti-LGBTQ Legislation Sweeping State Legislatures in 2021

So far in 2021, seventeen anti-LGBTQ bills have been enacted into law surpassing 2015 as the worst year for anti-LGBTQ legislation in recent history (when 15 anti-LGBTQ bills were enacted into law), including:

- 7 anti-trans sports bans in Arkansas, Alabama, Tennessee, Mississippi, Montana, and West Virginia
- 4 religious refusal bills, including in Arkansas, Montana, and South Dakota
- 2 anti-LGBTQ education bills in Tennessee and Montana
- 1 anti-trans medical care ban bill in Arkansas
- 1 sham "hate crimes" bill in Arkansas
- 1 anti-all comers bill in North Dakota
- 1 anti-trans birth certificate bill in Montana

With seventeen bills now signed into law, states have enacted more anti-LGBTQ laws this year than in the last three years combined (anti-LGBTQ bills enacted in previous years include 2 bills in 2018, 7 bills in 2019, and 4 bills in 2020).

More than 250 anti-LGBTQ bills have been introduced in state legislatures in 2021, including:

- At least 35 bills that would prohibit transgender youth from being able to access best-practice, age-appropriate, gender-affirming medical care
- At least 69 bills that would prohibit transgender youth (and in some cases college students) from participating in sports consistent with their gender identity
- At least 43 bills that would allow people to assert a religious belief as justification for failing to abide by the law or provide services to people of whom they disapprove
- At least 15 bills that would prohibit transgender people from having access to restrooms or locker rooms consistent with their gender identity

Wide Range of Business and Advocacy Groups, Athletes Oppose Anti-Trans Legislation

More than 90 major U.S. corporations have stood up and spoken out to oppose anti-transgender legislation being proposed in states across the country. New companies like Facebook, Pfizer, Altria, Peloton, and Dell join companies like Amazon, American Airlines, Apple, AT&T, AirBnB, Google, Hilton, IBM, IKEA, Microsoft, Nike, Paypal, Uber, and Verizon in objecting to these bills. Four of the largest U.S. food companies also condemned "dangerous, discriminatory legislation that serves as an attack on LGBTQ+ individuals, particularly transgender and nonbinary people," and the Walton Family Foundation issued a statement expressing "alarm" at the trend of anti-transgender legislation that has recently become law in Arkansas.

The nation's leading child health and welfare groups representing more than 7 million youth-serving professionals and more than 1,000 child welfare organizations released an open letter calling for lawmakers in states across the country to oppose dozens of bills that target LGBTQ people, and transgender children in particular.

A Fight Driven by National Anti-LGBTQ Groups, Not Local Legislators or Public Concern

These bills come from the same forces that drove previous anti-equality fights by pushing copycat bills across state houses—dangerous, anti-LGBTQ organizations like the Heritage Foundation, Alliance Defending Freedom (designated by Southern Poverty Law Center as a hate group), and Eagle Forum among others. For example, Montana's HB 112, the first anti-transgender sports bill to be passed in 2021 through a legislative chamber in any state, was worked on by the Alliance Defending Freedom.

Trans Equality Is Popular: Anti-Transgender Legislation Is a Low Priority, Even Among Trump Voters

- A new PBS/NPR/Marist poll states that 67% of Americans, including 66% of Republicans, oppose the anti-transgender sports ban legislation proliferating across 30 states.
- In a 10-swing-state poll conducted by the Human Rights Campaign & Hart Research Group last fall:
  - At least 60% of Trump voters across each of the 10 swing states say transgender people should be able to live freely and openly.
  - At least 87% of respondents across each of the 10 swing states say transgender people should have equal access to medical care, with many states breaking 90% support.
  - When respondents were asked about how they prioritized the importance of banning transgender people from participating in sports as compared to other policy issues, the issue came in dead last, with between 1% and 3% prioritizing the issue.
  - Another more recent poll conducted by the Human Rights Campaign & Hart Research Group revealed

that, with respect to transgender youth participation in sports, the public's strong inclination is on the side of fairness and equality for transgender student athletes. 73% of voters agree that "sports are important in young people's lives. Young transgender people should be allowed opportunities to participate in a way that is safe and comfortable for them."

States That Pass Anti-Transgender Legislation Suffer Economic, Legal, Reputational Harm

- Analyses conducted in the aftermath of previous divisive anti-transgender bills across the country, like the bathroom bills introduced in Texas and North Carolina and an anti-transgender sports ban in Idaho, show that there would be or has been devastating fallout.
- The Idaho anti-transgender sports bill that passed was swiftly suspended by a federal district court. The National Collegiate Athletic Association (NCAA) came out against the Idaho bill and others like it and subsequently moved planned tournament games out of Idaho.
- The Associated Press projected that the North Carolina bathroom bill could have cost the state $3.76 billion over 10 years.
- During a fight over an anti-transgender bathroom bill in 2017, the Texas Association of Business estimated $8.5 billion in economic losses, risking 185,000 jobs in the process due to National Collegiate Athletic Association (NCAA) and professional sporting event cancellations, a ban on taxpayer funded travel to those states, cancellation of movie productions, and businesses moving projects out of state.

VIEWPOINT

> "Attitudes on the acceptance of homosexuality are shaped by the country in which people live."

LGBTQIA+ Acceptance Differs Among Nations

Jacob Poushter and Nicholas Kent

In the previous viewpoint, the author pointed out research showing that solid majorities of Americans—on both sides of the political divide—oppose infringing on the rights of LGBTQIA+ people. Here, Jacob Poushter and Nicholas Kent take a look at the situation around the world. They found that the level of economic development, religious influence, and political attitudes all play a role in how supportive populations are of LGBTQIA+ rights. Jacob Poushter is associate director of Global Attitudes Research at Pew Research Center. At the time this viewpoint was published, Nicholas Kent was a research assistant focusing on global attitudes at Pew Research Center.

As you read, consider the following questions:

1. What are some examples of nations that have a high level of acceptance of LGBTQIA+ people? What do these nations have in common?

"The Global Divide on Homosexuality Persists," by Jacob Poushter and Nicholas Kent, Pew Research Center, June 25, 2020.

25

2. What are examples of nations that have a low acceptance of LGBTQIA+ people? What do these nations have in common?
3. In the countries where there is a difference in levels of LGBTQIA+ acceptance, who is most likely to be accepting of homosexuality, men or women? Younger people or older people?

Despite major changes in laws and norms surrounding the issue of same-sex marriage and the rights of LGBT people around the world, public opinion on the acceptance of homosexuality in society remains sharply divided by country, region and economic development.

As it was in 2013, when the question was last asked, attitudes on the acceptance of homosexuality are shaped by the country in which people live. Those in Western Europe and the Americas are generally more accepting of homosexuality than are those in Eastern Europe, Russia, Ukraine, the Middle East and sub-Saharan Africa. And publics in the Asia-Pacific region generally are split. This is a function not only of economic development of nations, but also religious and political attitudes.

But even with these sharp divides, views are changing in many of the countries that have been surveyed since 2002, when Pew Research Center first began asking this question. In many nations, there has been an increasing acceptance of homosexuality, including in the United States, where 72% say it should be accepted, compared with just 49% as recently as 2007.

Many of the countries surveyed in 2002 and 2019 have seen a double-digit increase in acceptance of homosexuality. This includes a 21-point increase since 2002 in South Africa and a 19-point increase in South Korea over the same time period. India also saw a 22-point increase since 2014, the first time the question was asked of a nationally representative sample there.

There also have been fairly large shifts in acceptance of homosexuality over the past 17 years in two very different places: Mexico and Japan. In both countries, just over half said they accepted homosexuality in 2002, but now closer to seven-in-ten say this.

In Kenya, only 1 in 100 said homosexuality should be accepted in 2002, compared with 14% who say this now.

In many of the countries surveyed, there also are differences on acceptance of homosexuality by age, education, income and, in some instances, gender—and in several cases, these differences are substantial. In addition, religion and its importance in people's lives shape opinions in many countries. For example, in some countries, those who are affiliated with a religious group tend to be less accepting of homosexuality than those who are unaffiliated (a group sometimes referred to as religious "nones").

Political ideology also plays a role in acceptance of homosexuality. In many countries, those on the political right are less accepting of homosexuality than those on the left. And supporters of several right-wing populist parties in Europe are also less likely to see homosexuality as acceptable.

Attitudes on this issue are strongly correlated with a country's wealth. In general, people in wealthier and more developed economies are more accepting of homosexuality than are those in less wealthy and developed economies.

For example, in Sweden, the Netherlands and Germany, all of which have a per-capita gross domestic product over $50,000, acceptance of homosexuality is among the highest measured across the 34 countries surveyed. By contrast, in Nigeria, Kenya and Ukraine, where per-capita GDP is under $10,000, less than two-in-ten say that homosexuality should be accepted by society.

These are among the major findings of a Pew Research Center survey conducted among 38,426 people in 34 countries from May 13 to Oct. 2, 2019. The study is a follow-up to a 2013 report that found many of the same patterns as seen today, although there has been an increase in acceptance of homosexuality across many of the countries surveyed in both years.

Varied Levels of Acceptance for Homosexuality Across Globe

The 2019 survey shows that while majorities in 16 of the 34 countries surveyed say homosexuality should be accepted by society, global divides remain. Whereas 94% of those surveyed in Sweden say homosexuality should be accepted, only 7% of people in Nigeria say the same. Across the 34 countries surveyed, a median of 52% agree that homosexuality should be accepted with 38% saying that it should be discouraged.

On a regional basis, acceptance of homosexuality is highest in Western Europe and North America. Central and Eastern Europeans, however, are more divided on the subject, with a median of 46% who say homosexuality should be accepted and 44% saying it should not be.

But in sub-Saharan Africa, the Middle East, Russia and Ukraine, few say that society should accept homosexuality; only in South Africa (54%) and Israel (47%) do more than a quarter hold this view.

People in the Asia-Pacific region show little consensus on the subject. More than three-quarters of those surveyed in Australia (81%) say homosexuality should be accepted, as do 73% of Filipinos. Meanwhile, only 9% in Indonesia agree.

In the three Latin American countries surveyed, strong majorities say they accept homosexuality in society.

Pew Research Center has been gathering data on acceptance of homosexuality in the U.S. since 1994, and there has been a relatively steady increase in the share who say that homosexuality should be accepted by society since 2000. However, while it took nearly 15 years for acceptance to rise 13 points from 2000 to just before the federal legalization of gay marriage in June 2015, there was a near equal rise in acceptance in just the four years *since* legalization.

What Is the Current State of LGBTQIA+ Rights?

While acceptance has increased over the past two decades, the partisan divide on homosexuality in the U.S. is wide. More than eight-in-ten Democrats and Democratic-leaning independents (85%) say homosexuality should be accepted, but only 58% of Republicans and Republican leaners say the same.

At the same time, the U.S. still maintains one of the lowest rates of acceptance among the Western European and North and South American countries surveyed. (For more on American views of homosexuality, LGBT issues and same-sex marriage, see Pew Research Center's topic page here; U.S. political and partisan views on this topic can be found here.)

In 22 of 34 countries surveyed, younger adults are significantly more likely than their older counterparts to say homosexuality should be accepted by society.

This difference was most pronounced in South Korea, where 79% of 18- to 29-year-olds say homosexuality should be accepted by society, compared with only 23% of those 50 and older. This staggering 56-point difference exceeds the next largest difference in Japan by 20 points, where 92% and 56% of those ages 18 to 29 and 50 and older, respectively, say homosexuality should be accepted by society.

In most of the countries surveyed, there are no significant differences between men and women. However, for all 12 countries surveyed where there was significant difference, women were more likely to approve of homosexuality than men. South Korea shows the largest divide, with 51% of women and 37% of men saying homosexuality should be accepted by society.

In most countries surveyed, those who have greater levels of education are significantly more likely to say that homosexuality should be accepted in society than those who have less education.[1]

For example, in Greece, 72% of those with a postsecondary education or more say homosexuality is acceptable, compared with 42% of those with a secondary education or less who say this. Significant differences of this nature are found in both countries with generally high levels of acceptance (such as Italy) and low levels (like Ukraine).

In a similar number of countries, those who earn more money than the country's national median income also are more likely to say they accept homosexuality in society than those who earn less. In Israel, for instance, 52% of higher income earners say homosexuality is acceptable in society versus only three-in-ten of lower income earners who say the same.

In many of the countries where there are measurements of ideology on a left-right scale, those on the left tend to be more accepting of homosexuality than those on the ideological right. And in many cases the differences are quite large.

In South Korea, for example, those who classify themselves on the ideological left are more than twice as likely to say homosexuality is acceptable than those on the ideological right (a 39-percentage-point difference). Similar double-digit differences of this nature appear in many European and North American countries.

In a similar vein, those who support right-wing populist parties in Europe, many of which are seen by LGBT groups as a threat to their rights, are less supportive of homosexuality in society. In Spain, people with a favorable opinion of the Vox party, which recently has begun to oppose some gay rights, are much less likely to say that homosexuality is acceptable than those who do not support the party.

And in Poland, supporters of the governing PiS (Law and Justice), which has explicitly targeted gay rights as anathema to traditional Polish values, are 23 percentage points less likely to say that homosexuality should be accepted by society than those who do not support the governing party.

Similar differences appear in neighboring Hungary, where the ruling Fidesz party, led by Prime Minister Viktor Orbán, also has shown hostility to gay rights. But even in countries like France and Germany where acceptance of homosexuality is high, there are differences between supporters and non-supporters of key right-wing populist parties such as National Rally in France and Alternative for Germany (AfD).

Religion, both as it relates to relative importance in people's lives and actual religious affiliation, also plays a large role in perceptions of the acceptability of homosexuality in many societies across the globe.

In 25 of the 34 countries surveyed, those who say religion is "somewhat," "not too" or "not at all" important in their lives are more likely to say that homosexuality should be accepted than those who say religion is "very" important. Among Israelis, those who say religion is not very important in their lives are almost three times more likely than those who say religion is very important to say that society should accept homosexuality.

Significant differences of this nature appear across a broad spectrum of both highly religious and less religious countries, including Czech Republic (38-percentage-point difference), South Korea (38), Canada (33), the U.S. (29), Slovakia (29), Greece (28) and Turkey (26).

Religious affiliation also plays a key role in views towards acceptance of homosexuality. For example, those who are religiously unaffiliated, sometimes called religious "nones," (that is, those who identify as atheist, agnostic or "nothing in particular") tend to be more accepting of homosexuality. Though the opinions of religiously unaffiliated people can vary widely, in virtually every country surveyed with a sufficient number of unaffiliated respondents, "nones" are more accepting of homosexuality than the affiliated. In most cases, the affiliated comparison group is made up of Christians. But even among Christians, Catholics are more likely to accept homosexuality than Protestants and evangelicals in many countries with enough adherents for analysis.

One example of this pattern can be found in South Korea. Koreans who are religiously unaffiliated are about twice as likely to say that homosexuality should be accepted by society (60%) as those who are Christian (24%) or Buddhist (31%). Similarly, in

Hungary, 62% of "nones" say society should accept homosexuality, compared with only 48% of Catholics.

In the few countries surveyed with Muslim populations large enough for analysis, acceptance of homosexuality is particularly low among adherents of Islam. But in Nigeria, for example, acceptance of homosexuality is low among Christians and Muslims alike (6% and 8%, respectively). Jews in Israel are much more likely to say that homosexuality is acceptable than Israeli Muslims (53% and 17%, respectively).

Endnote

1. For the purpose of comparing educational groups across countries, we standardize education levels based on the UN's International Standard Classification of Education (ISCED). The lower education category is below secondary education and the higher category is secondary or above in Brazil, India, Indonesia, Kenya, Lebanon, Mexico, Nigeria, the Philippines, South Africa, Tunisia and Ukraine. In all other countries, the lower education category is secondary education or less education and the higher category is postsecondary or more education.

Viewpoint 3

> "Trans women candidates were enormously successful at the ballot box—outperforming candidates of all other gender identities and further highlighting the disconnect between voters and the politicians who promote anti-trans agendas."

U.S. Voters Are Increasingly Willing to Elect LGBTQIA+ Candidates

Los Angeles Blade

As a significant percentage of the total population in the U.S., LGBTQIA+ people are still very much under-represented in elected office. However, this viewpoint from the Los Angeles Blade points out some promising news for LGBTQIA+ candidates: Americans are increasingly willing to elect LGBTQIA+ representatives. This suggests that politicians and interest groups who promote an anti-LGBTQIA+ agenda are not having much luck with the general population of voters, and in the future, it is likely that LGBTQIA+ people will gain more representation in politics. The Los Angeles Blade *is Los Angeles' LGBTQIA+ newspaper covering the latest gay, lesbian, bisexual, and transgender news in Southern California and around the world.*

"184 LGBTQ Candidates Won Elected Office in 2021," Los Angeles Blade. Reprinted by permission.

LGBTQIA+ Rights

As you read, consider the following questions:

1. What group of LGBTQIA+ candidates had the best success rate?
2. According to reporting in this viewpoint, what do the results say about the disconnect between anti-gay politicians and voters?
3. According to this viewpoint, what percentage of the U.S. population is LGBTQIA+?

At least 184 out LGBTQ candidates won elected office throughout 2021, more than in any other odd-numbered election year in U.S. history. The previous record was 169 candidates set in 2019. Transgender women won 63 percent of their races—the highest win rate of any gender identity—followed by cisgender women candidates, who won 51 percent of their races.

Of the 184 LGBTQ candidates who won, 112 were non-incumbents, and 73 of 89 incumbents won. When the newly elected officials take office, there will be approximately 1,038 serving out LGBTQ elected officials in the U.S.—surpassing 1,000 for the first time. There are currently 995 out elected officials serving.

Below are key findings and a demographic and success breakdown of the 430 known out LGBTQ candidates who ran in 2021—looking at sexual orientation, gender identity, race/ethnicity, incumbency and endorsement status. A statement from Mayor Annise Parker, President & CEO of LGBTQ Victory Fund, is also included below.

Key findings from the data include:

- 46 percent of known out LGBTQ candidates won their races in 2021, including 59 percent of Victory Fund endorsed candidates;*
- Trans women had the highest win rates of any gender identity (63 percent), with 12 trans women winning their elections;
- Lesbian candidates outperformed all other sexual orientation groups, winning 60 percent of their elections;

- Cisgender women outperformed cisgender men by seven percentage points—51 percent compared to 44 percent;
- 37 percent of LGBTQ candidates in 2021 were people of color and 37 percent won their races—with Asian and Pacific Islander candidates winning 58 percent of races; and
- A historic number of non-binary (16) and queer-identified people (53) ran, but their win rates were 28 percent and 35 percent, respectively.

"Trans women candidates were enormously successful at the ballot box—outperforming candidates of all other gender identities and further highlighting the disconnect between voters and the politicians who promote anti-trans agendas," said Mayor Annise Parker, President & CEO of LGBTQ Victory Fund. "Beyond that notable exception, LGBTQ candidates who face the most structural barriers were often those who struggled most at the ballot box. But many are first time candidates who will run again and the experiences from this year will be invaluable in their next campaign."

"While more LGBTQ candidates won election in 2021 than in any other odd-numbered election year, the growth is modest compared to how far we are from achieving equitable representation. As anti-LGBTQ politicians introduce hundreds of hateful bills and extreme right-wing activists attack trans students in school board meetings, it is imperative we elect more LGBTQ people to counter their efforts. There is no better weapon than an LGBTQ elected official who can humanize our issues and lives for their legislative colleagues and constituents."

When the newly elected officials take office, LGBTQ people will hold just 0.2 percent of all elected positions in the United States, despite representing at least 5.6 percent of the U.S. population. Currently LGBTQ elected officials hold just 0.19 percent of positions.

The LGBTQIA+ Community Is Underrepresented in Elected Office

As of 2021, 5.6 percent of Americans identify as LGBTQ+; however, only two Senators and nine Representatives (a cumulative 2.1 percent of the 117th Congress) currently identify this way. Four of the eleven openly LGBTQ+ members of Congress are female (two Senators, two Representatives).

The November 2020 election saw many first for LGBTQ+ candidate firsts at the state and local levels, to learn more about some of the winners on our Milestones page.

Unless greater numbers of LGBTQ+ people are elected to office, LGBTQ+ underrepresentation will only become more pronounced: according to recent Gallup polling, one in six adults from Generation Z identify as LGBTQ+. More openly LGBTQ+ representatives must be elected in order to accurately represent a growing population of LGBTQ+ constituents.

In 2021, the LGBTQ Victory Institute released a groundbreaking study on the barriers and motivators experienced by LGBTQ women considering a run for office. Notably, one of the barriers listed refers to the lack of LGBTQ women represented in office currently.

As important as descriptive representation is for the sake democracy, having representatives in office who substantively share in the lived-experiences of their constituents (and political hopefuls) is just as important. For LGBTQ women considering a run for office, these "trailblazers" may present themselves as mentors who can answer specific questions about running for office, while also alleviating concerns about the viability of their own campaigns.

In 1998, Tammy Baldwin (D-WI) became the first openly lesbian person elected to the House of Representatives, and she became the first openly gay or lesbian person elected to the Senate in 2012. The same year, Kyrsten Sinema (D-AZ) was elected as the first openly bisexual member of the House of Representatives.

No transgender person has ever been elected to the U.S. Senate or House of Representatives. The first transgender member of a state legislature, Althea Garrison, was elected in Massachusetts in 1992, though her gender identity was not widely known during her campaign. In 2008, Stu Rasmussen was elected mayor of Silverton, Oregon, becoming the first openly transgender mayor elected in the U.S.

What Is the Current State of LGBTQIA+ Rights?

Oregon Governor Kate Brown became the first openly bisexual governor when she was appointed to the position in 2015, and was elected in her own right in 2016.

In 2019, Sharice Davids (D, KS-03) became the first LGBTQ+ Native American in the U.S. House of Representatives.

"The LGBT Community Remains Underrepresented in Elected Office," RepresentWomen, November 2021.

Win/Loss Breakdown of the 430 Out LGBTQ Candidates Who Ran in 2021

NOTE: Win rates are calculated using candidates who appeared on the ballot and do not include candidates who dropped out before their election or are still in runoffs.

2021 LGBTQ CANDIDATES	2021 TOTAL	WINS	LOSSES	TO RUNOFF	DROPPED/ WITHDREW	% WON*
VICTORY FUND ENDORSED LGBTQ CANDIDATES	176	103	72	1	0	58.9%
NON-ENDORSED LGBTQ CANDIDATES	254	81	141	2	30	36.2%
ALL LGBTQ CANDIDATES	430	184	213	3	30	46.3%

INCUMBENCY	2021 TOTAL	WINS	LOSSES	TO RUNOFF	DROPPED/ WITHDREW	% WON*
INCUMBENTS	89	72	16	1	0	80.9%
NON-INCUMBENT	341	112	197	2	30	36.0%
ALL LGBTQ CANDIDATES	430	184	213	3	30	46.3%

OFFICE LEVEL	2021 TOTAL	WINS	LOSSES	TO RUNOFF	DROPPED/ WITHDREW	% WON*
FEDERAL	3	0	2	0	1	0%
STATEWIDE	3	0	2	0	1	0%
STATE LEGISLATURE	20	6	14	0	0	30%
JUDICIAL	7	5	2	0	0	71.4%
MAYOR	41	16	22	1	2	41.0%
LOCAL (NOT INCL. MAYOR)	356	157	171	2	26	47.6%
ALL LGBTQ CANDIDATES	430	184	213	3	30	46.3%

LGBTQIA+ Rights

GENDER IDENTITY	2021 TOTAL	WINS	LOSSES	TO RUNOFF	DROPPED/ WITHDREW	% WON*
AGENDER	1	0	1	0	0	0%
CISGENDER MEN	235	95	122	2	16	43.78%
CISGENDER WOMEN	118	59	56	0	3	51.3%
GENDER NON-CONFORMING	6	2	3	1	0	40.0%
INTERSEX	0	0	0	0	0	0%
NON-BINARY / GENDERQUEER	19	5	13	0	1	27.8%
TRANS MEN	6	2	4	0	0	33.3%
TRANS WOMEN	21	12	7	0	2	63.2%
TRANS NON-BINARY	1	0	1	0	0	0%
TWO SPIRIT	1	0	1	0	0	0%
OTHER	1	0	1	0	0	0%
UNKNOWN	21	9	4	0	8	69.2%
ALL LGBTQ CANDIDATES	**430**	**184**	**213**	**3**	**30**	**46.3%**

SEXUAL ORIENTATION	2021 TOTAL	WINS	LOSSES	TO RUNOFF	DROPPED/ WITHDREW	% WON*
ASEXUAL	2	0	2	0	0	0.0%
BISEXUAL	41	18	22	1	0	45.0%
GAY	192	88	90	1	13	45.8%

VIEWPOINT 4

> "[This decision] suggests that when the broader question of whether religious groups have the right to discriminate does come before the justices, they will likely uphold religious liberty over gay rights."

High Court Ruling Does Not Bode Well for LGBTQIA+ Rights

Morgan Marietta

In this viewpoint, Morgan Marietta discusses a Supreme Court ruling that favored a Catholic adoption agency that did not work with same-sex couples and was excluded from Philadelphia's foster programs as a result. Though the details are fairly technical, the ruling has a potentially momentous impact for the future of LGBTQIA+ rights. Here, the author argues that this decision heralds more limits to LGBTQIA+ protections, with the Supreme Court favoring religious liberty over LGBTQIA+ rights. Morgan Marietta is an associate professor of political science at the University of Massachusetts Lowell. His research focuses on the political consequences of belief.

"Supreme Court Unanimously Upholds Religious Liberty over LGBTQ Rights—and Nods to a Bigger Win for Conservatives Ahead," by Morgan Marietta, The Conversation, June 18, 2021. https://theconversation.com/supreme-court-unanimously-upholds-religious-liberty-over-lgbtq-rights-and-nods-to-a-bigger-win-for-conservatives-ahead-161398. Licensed under CC BY 4.0 International.

LGBTQIA+ Rights

As you read, consider the following questions:

1. What does the author mean when he says that this ruling is "narrow?"
2. What was the city of Philadelphia's argument in this case?
3. What did the separate opinions signed by Justices Samuel Alito, Neil Gorsuch, and Clarence Thomas say?

It wasn't a dramatic expansion of religious rights—not yet. But the Supreme Court's ruling in favor of a Catholic adoption agency that had been excluded from Philadelphia's foster programs for refusing to work with same-sex couples will be consequential. It suggests that when the broader question of whether religious groups have the right to discriminate does come before the justices, they will likely uphold religious liberty over gay rights.

The court's decision, delivered in a 9-0 ruling, emphasizes a pluralist approach: The Christian agency gets to participate in the adoption programs while adhering to its religious beliefs, and LGBTQ couples will continue to have access to other adoption agencies within the Philadelphia system.

The ruling is narrow, but it means that any unequal treatment of religious groups will be regarded as a violation of the First Amendment, even if it comes at the expense of the dignity of LGBTQ citizens.

Perhaps the most important aspect of the ruling is its unanimity in upholding a clear standard of neutral treatment for religious and secular groups. The city government claimed it was not violating this standard, but even the liberal justices agreed it was.

The city's contention that government funding or the city's contracting rules shifted the equation against religious rights was roundly rejected by the court.

The unanimous ruling was achieved by delaying another core question that some of the justices wanted to address: whether religious businesses or groups have the clear right to deny service to the LGBTQ community or whether states can insist that in the public square, such faith-based groups set aside discriminatory beliefs.

Nonetheless, as a scholar of the Supreme Court, I believe the decision of the nine justices will have broad ramifications for current government policies and future judicial rulings. By subordinating the dignity of same-sex couples to the religious rights of believers, the court's new decisive ruling will influence many interactions between religious organizations and LGBTQ citizens.

Harming the Dignity of Same-Sex Couples

The case in front of the Supreme Court addressed the city of Philadelphia's refusal to continue to allow Catholic Social Services to participate in the city's adoption and foster programs because the religious charity would not serve same-sex couples.

The group claimed that its First Amendment right to free exercise of religion had been violated as a result.

The organization, along with Sharonell Fulton and Toni Simms-Busch—two Catholic women who wished to serve as foster parents through the agency—sued the city.

They were aided by the Becket Fund for Religious Liberty, a nonprofit law firm behind several successful Supreme Court cases, including 2014's *Burwell v. Hobby Lobby*, which upheld the ability of religious businesses to refuse to pay for forms of contraception that violate their beliefs, and *Little Sisters of the Poor v. Pennsylvania* in 2021, which also protected religious exemptions to contraceptive coverage under the Affordable Care Act.

The city of Philadelphia argued that religious rights do not allow for harms to third parties, including to the dignity of the same-sex couples being told publicly that they are not acceptable.

As one constitutional law professor wrote in an amicus brief in favor of the city: "The believers can believe whatever they like and organize their affairs through discriminatory purposes, to be sure, but not when the government is paying and not when the public is impacted."

But the justices seem to have agreed with the alternative framing offered by Lori Windham, the advocate for Fulton: "Does the Free Exercise clause shrink every time the government expands its reach and begins to regulate work that has historically and traditionally been done by religious groups?"

A Surprising Unanimity

All nine justices agreed with the core holding that Philadelphia could not exclude Catholic Social Services. There were no dissents from Justices Stephen Breyer, Elena Kagan or Sonia Sotomayor—the current liberal wing of the court.

But three of the conservative justices—Samuel Alito, Neil Gorsuch and Clarence Thomas—signed separate opinions agreeing with the outcome but arguing that the protections of religious rights should have been even stronger.

The ruling does not protect the ability of religious groups to discriminate or exclude under any circumstances. Rather, it prevents government authorities only from applying different standards to religious and secular organizations. Philadelphia's policies did not apply a "generally applicable" rule, but instead allow exceptions at their discretion.

In coming to their decision, the justices cited previous decisions holding that if government allows exceptions for secular reasons, then the First Amendment demands that they also allow them for religious reasons. As Chief Justice John Roberts phrased it, "The creation of a formal mechanism for granting exceptions renders a policy not generally applicable."

In presenting the case to the justices, Fulton's attorney argued: "In our pluralistic society, this Court has repeatedly said that there should be room for those with different views."

Roberts' majority opinion appears to reflect that view: "No same-sex couple has ever sought certification from CSS. If one did, CSS would direct the couple to one of the more than 20 other agencies in the City, all of which currently certify same-sex couples."

For this reason, "CSS seeks only an accommodation that will allow it to continue serving the children of Philadelphia in a manner consistent with its religious beliefs; it does not seek to impose those beliefs on anyone else."

The Expansion of Religious Rights

At a mere 15 pages, the ruling is what Justice Alito described as a "wisp of a decision" in his 77-page concurrence. He argued that the court should have decided more boldly in favor of expanded religious rights.

The Fulton decision follows a long string of other rulings that have tipped in favor of religious claimants. In recent years, the court has increasingly protected the freedom of religious groups in government programs, in commerce, in public displays and in public school programs.

The most recent ruling also suggests the limits of LGBTQ rights under the current court. There have been no major victories on this issue at the Supreme Court since the 2018 retirement of Justice Anthony Kennedy—the author of every major gay rights ruling in recent decades including *Obergefell v. Hodges*, which legalized same-sex marriage throughout the country in 2015. But Kennedy himself hinted at the limits to LGBTQ rights when they are in opposition to religious liberties, writing in the Obergefell decision that "the First Amendment ensures that religious organizations and persons are given proper protection as they seek to teach the principles that are so fulfilling and so central to their lives and faiths."

Since the Obergefell case, most of the Supreme Court cases addressing LGBTQ rights have not been brought by an LGBTQ plaintiff. Instead, they have been brought—and won—by religious groups.

The Question to Come

The Fulton case proved no exception to this winning streak for religious rights.

But what the ruling did not do is hand down a definitive answer to the question that these cases are moving toward: Should gay rights or religious rights yield when the two are in irreconcilable conflict? When the court answers that question, it will likely not be unanimous. But the current trajectory suggests that religious rights are more likely to prevail.

As Justice Gorsuch concluded in his concurring opinion, "dodging the question today guarantees it will recur tomorrow."

VIEWPOINT 5

> "The United States in recent years has become a leading advocate for LGBTQ+ rights internationally. U.S. credibility on the issue, though, is intrinsically tied to the country's own fight for equality and representation in government."

Protection of LGBTQIA+ Rights Has an Uneven History

Paul J. Angelo and Dominic Bocci

A previous viewpoint looked at worldwide attitudes toward LGBTQIA+ rights. In this viewpoint, Paul J. Angelo and Dominic Bocci zero in on the details of LGBTQIA+ discrimination and the uneven role of the United States in defending and expanding LGBTQIA+ rights, both domestically and in international relations. They also discuss the challenges U.S. leaders face in this area. Paul J. Angelo is director of the William J. Perry Center for Hemispheric Defense Studies at the National Defense University. Dominic Bocci is director of grant management at the Council of Foreign Relations.

As you read, consider the following questions:

1. According to this viewpoint, what sorts of discrimination do LGBTQIA+ people face around the world?

"The Changing Landscape of Global LGBTQ+ Rights", by Paul J. Angelo and Dominic Bocci, The Council on Foreign Relations, January 29, 2021. Reprinted by permission.

2. What advances and setbacks has the United States made in this area in recent decades?
3. This viewpoint—which was written in 2021, early in the Biden administration—mentions challenges Biden faced in protecting LGBTQIA+ rights. What were some of these challenges?

The global campaign to secure protections for lesbian, gay, bisexual, transgender, queer, and other (LGBTQ+) people has made significant progress in recent decades, especially in the realm of marriage equality. Yet in many countries, LGBTQ+ individuals still face repression, imprisonment, and even the threat of death. Given the severity and ubiquity of such abuses, laws and safeguards protecting this community from legal discrimination and political, social, and economic marginalization have become a priority for activists and a growing number of governments.

The United States has long been an important battleground for LGBTQ+ rights, and U.S. leadership has been prominent in defending them worldwide. However, a rapid expansion of protections in the United States during the Barack Obama administration was stalled—or, in areas such as health care and military service, even reversed—by the Donald J. Trump administration. Trump also deprioritized the promotion of LGBTQ+ rights in U.S. foreign policy.

This erosion of the U.S. global standing on human rights issues poses an initial challenge for President Joe Biden, who is expected to pursue robust LGBTQ+ rights advocacy. Biden is likely to face resistance from conservative lawmakers and judges, but his commitment to using executive powers—evident in the signing of an executive order on his first day in office to protect LGBTQ+ Americans from discrimination—bodes well for the restoration of the United States' standing as a global leader in the defense of such rights.

Progress and Pitfalls in Global Rights

Civil society organizations have lobbied the United Nations for recognition of human rights on the basis of sexual orientation and gender identity since the body's founding in 1945. However, it was not until the 1994 *Toonen v. Australia* case, brought before the UN Human Rights Committee, that the discrimination of individuals based on their sexual orientation became a recognized violation in international human rights law. In 2007, as case law in the area slowly evolved and instances of LGBTQ+ human rights violations garnered increased publicity, a group of independent experts met in Indonesia to articulate clear guidance for international human rights standards and their application to issues related to sexual orientation. Their efforts produced the Yogyakarta Principles, which have served as a touchstone for LGBTQ+ rights ever since.

In 2011, U.S. Secretary of State Hillary Clinton marshalled support in the UN Human Rights Council, the successor to the Human Rights Committee, for the resolution on human rights, sexual orientation, and gender identity, famously proclaiming that "gay rights are human rights." In 2016, the council adopted another resolution that called on member states to protect against violence and discrimination based on sexual orientation and gender identity and established the office of an independent expert to assess implementation of these protections worldwide.

Yet, such protections are unevenly enshrined in law throughout the world, and anti-LGBTQ+ discrimination persists. Around seventy countries continue to criminalize homosexual activity, and in twelve countries adults who engage in consensual same-sex acts can still face the death penalty. In countries such as Afghanistan, Pakistan, and Qatar, these measures tend not to be enforced even if they are legally permissible, but Iran still regularly executes LGBTQ+ individuals. Additionally, in geographic areas beyond the reach of governments, terrorist organizations such as the self-proclaimed Islamic State perpetrate anti-LGBTQ+ violence.

Even where same-sex sexual activity is not illegal, officials often overlook abuse and murder of LGBTQ+ individuals perpetrated by law enforcement officers, militant groups, street gangs, and even their own family members. Forced marriages, so-called honor killings, and the use of rape as a way of "undoing" a victim's sexual orientation or gender identity continue to jeopardize lives in places where state capacity is limited. Transgender people are especially vulnerable to these acts of violence. In some Catholic- and Muslim-majority states with a history of authoritarianism, conservative interpretations of religious texts are often used to ostracize sexual minorities and justify discrimination against them. In Central America, for instance, LGBTQ+ people face structural discrimination, persecution, and high susceptibility to homicide, resulting in a recent surge of LGBTQ+ people seeking asylum in the United States.

A mere twenty-nine countries legally recognize marriage equality today, including Switzerland most recently with its December 2020 passage of marriage equality legislation. And even among countries where same-sex marriage is legal, some still lag behind in protecting LGBTQ+ people from discrimination in access to social and commercial services, education, health, and employment; only eleven countries mention sexual orientation in constitutional nondiscrimination clauses. European countries stand out for extending protection under Article 21 of the European Union Charter of Fundamental Rights and Article 19 of the Treaty on the Functioning of the EU, but LGBTQ+ rights are increasingly under assault on the continent.

In Poland and Hungary, the use of homophobic rhetoric and legislation by reactionary political parties that have recently assumed power prompted the European Commission in 2020 to deny some funding to member states that do not respect LGBTQ+ rights and to take steps toward including homophobic hate crimes on a list of major offenses.

Advances at Home Reflected in U.S. Foreign Policy

Against this difficult panorama, the United States in recent years has become a leading advocate for LGBTQ+ rights internationally. U.S. credibility on the issue, though, is intrinsically tied to the country's own fight for equality and representation in government.

LGBTQ+ Americans historically faced legal and social discrimination, including regarding the right to serve in the military, work in the civil service, and represent the country abroad. During the Cold War, LGBTQ+ individuals were systematically purged from government service, and the federal government continued denying security clearances on the basis of sexual orientation until the early 1990s. Furthermore, in 1993, the Department of Defense issued Instruction 1304.26 to authorize the discharge of LGBTQ+ military personnel who disclosed their sexual orientation—a policy that effectively closeted service members and became known as the "Don't Ask, Don't Tell" policy.

Meanwhile, a new generation of activists emerged in the 1980s to contest government inaction and growing stigmatization in the face of the HIV/AIDS crisis, which disproportionately affected LGBTQ+ communities around the globe. In the United States, activist pressure put an end to legal discrimination against HIV/AIDS patients, forced the U.S. government's hand in allocating resources for treatment research, and increased public awareness by creating the policy and educational infrastructure for civil society to continue organizing around LGBTQ+ rights.

The Obama administration represented a turning point in U.S. policy, making LGBTQ+ rights central to both its domestic and foreign policy agendas. In addition to repealing restrictions on military service, it improved access to health services for transgender people by including transgender health coverage under the Affordable Care Act. Obama also prioritized legislation to prevent bullying and hate crimes against LGBTQ+ Americans, extended same-sex domestic partner benefits for those working in executive branch departments, and signed an executive order protecting LGBTQ+ employees working for government contractors nationwide. In 2012, Obama became the first U.S. president to voice his support for same-sex marriage, which was ultimately legalized nationwide by the U.S. Supreme Court in 2015.

The Obama administration emerged as a world leader in advocacy, helping set the UN agenda for expanded international protections for LGBTQ+ people; launching the State Department's Global Equality Fund to advance their human rights around the world; and directing executive agencies to promote these rights in diplomacy and foreign assistance, including through encouraging the repeal of discriminatory laws. In 2015, Obama appointed the first-ever special envoy for LGBTQ+ human rights to coordinate U.S. diplomacy on the matter.

Trump's Reversal of LGBTQ+ Protections

The Trump administration's approach to LGBTQ+ rights involved appointing several openly gay men to high-ranking diplomatic and national security positions and overseeing a largely rhetorical campaign to decriminalize homosexuality worldwide, which fell short of its objectives. At the same time, Trump repealed many critical protections. He initiated, by tweet, a ban on military service for transgender service members and rolled back healthcare guarantees for transgender patients. His administration also launched the Commission on Unalienable Rights, which threatened LGBTQ+ and women's rights under the guise of religious liberty despite claiming to protect human rights.

During his final days in office, Trump adopted rules that permit recipients of grants from the Department of Health and Human Services to discriminate against LGBTQ+ people, affecting services including foster care and adoption, refugee assistance, and HIV prevention. Trump's foreign policy agenda de-emphasized the inclusion and advocacy at the heart of Obama-era diplomacy, even removing references to LGBTQ+ people from policy guidance.

Yet, global advancements in equality for LGBTQ+ individuals continued, largely without U.S. leadership. In 2017, the United Nations appointed its second independent expert on sexual orientation and gender identity, who in 2019 published a report calling for a global ban on conversion therapies—widespread practices based on a belief that a person's sexuality and gender can and should be changed to conform to heterosexual and cisgender norms. Furthermore, in 2017, Ireland elected its first openly gay prime minister, shortly followed by the election of Serbia's first openly lesbian and first female prime minister. Scores of openly LGBTQ+ candidates were elected to major public offices in countries such as Colombia and Japan. Even Pope Francis expressed support for LGBTQ+ individuals and their right to same-sex civil unions, though Vatican officials say such views reflect his personal beliefs and do not represent a change in church doctrine, which still prohibits same-sex marriage.

Challenges and Opportunities for Biden

Joe Biden campaigned for president on a promise to restore the United States' standing as a leader in defending the rights of LGBTQ+ individuals. Given his recent record in this area—including being the first senior Obama administration official to back marriage equality and arguing in international forums that LGBTQ+ issues are the civil rights issue of our time—Biden is poised to make advancements in this space.

Biden has vowed to work closely with allies and like-minded governments to ensure that violence and discrimination against LGBTQ+ individuals do not go unchecked. The Biden administration could, for instance, confront illiberal crackdowns in Eastern and Central Europe and targeted harassment by law enforcement in the Middle East, North Africa, and sub-Saharan Africa with sanctions, while also expanding asylum protections for LGBTQ+ individuals seeking refuge in the United States.

Domestically, Biden fulfilled a promise to overturn the ban on military service for transgender people during his first week in office and has committed to reinstating antidiscrimination policies in federal contracting. Today, LGBTQ+ Americans in some U.S. states still struggle to secure housing and access to employment benefits. Both President Biden and Vice President Kamala Harris have publicly committed their support to the Equality Act, legislation that would provide federal protection against all anti-LGBTQ+ discrimination. Efforts in this area will largely depend on congressional backing but seem achievable given increasing support for LGBTQ+ rights among the broader public.

Further, the administration promises to reflect the diversity of the United States in its staffing, strengthening recognition of LGBTQ+ professionals through appointments to senior domestic policy and national security positions. The president has already nominated Pete Buttigieg, the former mayor of South Bend, Indiana, to lead the Department of Transportation, which would make Buttigieg the first openly gay cabinet member if confirmed by the Senate. Biden has also put forth Rachel Levine as his choice for assistant secretary for health—the first-ever transgender individual to receive a nomination to a Senate-confirmed position—and is likely to name the first openly lesbian U.S. ambassador.

Biden will face a full slate of domestic and foreign policy challenges during the first one hundred days of his presidency. But having made clear that LGBTQ+ rights will be a top priority, Biden recognizes that restoring U.S. credibility to defend and advance human rights abroad starts with the United States' own commitment to guaranteeing LGBTQ+ rights at home.

VIEWPOINT 6

> *"It's important to understand that the bipartisan support for this bill marks a significant political transformation on same-sex marriage, which was used as a contentious point separating Democrats and Republicans roughly 15 to 20 years ago."*

Acceptance of Same-Sex Marriage Has Increased Over Time

Tim Lindberg

In this viewpoint, Tim Lindberg looks at the history of attitudes toward same-sex marriage among the American public and politicians, which have changed considerably in recent decades. This viewpoint was published just before the Respect for Marriage Act was passed by Congress and signed into law by President Joe Biden on December 13, 2022, which ensures that the federal government and state governments will recognize same-sex marriages. As Lindberg explains, a national shift in attitudes toward same-sex marriage began in 2012, when then-Vice President Biden and then-President Barack Obama supported it after having opposed it in the past. Former President Trump's inattention to the issue also helped it

"How Same-Sex Marriage Gained Bipartisan Support—a Decades-Long Process Has Brought It Close to Being Written into Federal Law," by Tim Lindberg, The Conversation, November 17, 2022. https://theconversation.com/how-same-sex-marriage-gained-bipartisan-support-a-decadeslong-process-has-brought-it-close-to-being-written-into-federal-law-194879. Licensed under CC BY-ND 4.0 International.

53

LGBTQIA+ Rights

become less divisive. Tim Lindberg is an assistant professor of political science at the University of Minnesota.

As you read, consider the following questions:

1. According to data from a Gallup poll cited in this viewpoint, what percentage of Americans supported same-sex marriage in 2022? How does this compare to poll results from 1996?
2. What president signed the Defense of Marriage Act—which the Respect for Marriage Act repealed—into law?
3. How many moderate Republican senators voted to advance the Respect for Marriage Act?

While public opinion and different state laws on abortion rights are sharply dividing the country, there's growing indication that most people agree on another once-controversial topic—protecting same-sex marriage.

The U.S. Senate voted on Nov. 16, 2022, to initiate debate on legislation that would protect same-sex and interracial marriage, making it legal regardless of where these couples live and what state laws determine.

Senators voted 62-37 to move forward on a final vote for the Respect for Marriage Act, with 12 Republicans joining Democrats in their support for the bill.

The legislation would also repeal the 1996 Defense of Marriage Act, a federal law that defines marriage as the legal union between a man and a woman.

The U.S. House of Representatives already voted on July 19, 2022, to enshrine same-sex marriage into law with a bipartisan vote—all 220 Democratic representatives voted in favor, joined by 47 Republican colleagues.

I am a scholar of political behavior and history in the U.S. I believe that it's important to understand that the bipartisan support for this bill marks a significant political transformation on same-sex marriage, which was used as a contentious point separating Democrats and Republicans roughly 15 to 20 years ago.

But over the past several years, same-sex marriage has become less politically divisive and gained more public approval, driven in part by former President Donald Trump's general acceptance of the practice. This environment made it politically safe for nearly a quarter of Republican House members to vote to protect this right under federal law.

What Makes Opinions Change?

Seventy-one percent of Americans say they support legal same-sex marriage, according to a July 2022 Gallup poll. In 1996, when Gallup first polled about same-sex marriage, 27% supported legalization of same-sex marriage.

This shift in public opinion has happened despite increasing polarization in the U.S. about gun control, racial justice and climate change.

What becomes, remains or ceases to be a divisive political issue in the U.S. over time depends on many factors. Changes to laws, shifting cultural norms and technological progress can all shape political controversies.

My research, for example, explores how Mormons in Utah territory—what would later become Utah state—were denied statehood by Congress until they gave up their religious belief in polygamy. Polygamy was outlawed under U.S. law, and known polygamists were excluded from voting and holding office. In the 1880s, an estimated 20% to 30% of Mormons practiced polygamy. Yet, political pressure led the Mormon Church president in 1890 to announce that polygamy would no longer be sanctioned.

In 2011, 86% of Mormon adults reported that they consider polygamy morally wrong, nearly in line with general public opinion.

Many political leaders, both on the left and right, were also largely hostile to same-sex marriage until the early 2010s.

A Rising Controversy

In 1993, the Hawaii Supreme Court ruled that the state must have a compelling reason to ban same-sex marriage, after a gay male couple and two lesbian couples filed a suit that a state ban on same-sex marriage violated their privacy and equal protection rights.

Concern among conservatives that this legal reasoning would lead the Supreme Court to acknowledge a right to same-sex marriage led to a Republican Senator and Congressman introducing the Defense of Marriage Act.

President Bill Clinton signed the bill in 1996 after 342—or 78%—of House members and 85 senators voted for it. Polling at the time showed support among the general population for same-sex marriage was 27% overall, including just 33% among Democrats.

Seven years later, in 2003, the Massachusetts Supreme Court struck down a state ban on same-sex marriage. With a strong majority nationally of Republicans and independents opposed to same-sex marriage, former President George W. Bush used conservative reactions to that decision to encourage voter turnout in 2004. Bush's campaign highlighted state amendments to ban same-sex marriage, all of which easily passed.

Although voters prioritized other issues in the 2004 elections, the opposition to same-sex marriage helped Bush win reelection, while Republicans picked up seats in both the House and Senate.

A Political Change

The legal and political landscape on same-sex marriage became much more liberal in the years following 2004.

In 2008, state courts in California and Connecticut struck down bans on same-sex marriage. Vermont became the first state in 2009 to pass legislation and legalize same-sex marriage.

A major national shift occurred in 2012 when then-Vice President Joe Biden and President Barack Obama openly supported same-sex marriage. This was a major change for both men. Biden had voted in favor of the Defense of Marriage Act in 1996. Obama publicly supported marriage as being between a man and a woman in his 2004 senatorial campaign.

In 2015, the Supreme Court struck down all national and state restrictions on same-sex marriage, making same-sex marriage the law of the land.

The Trump Effect

The lack of attention Trump paid to same-sex marriage is one factor that contributed to it becoming a less divisive issue. While Trump's actual record on LBGTQ rights generally aligns with conservative Christian values, Trump had said in 2016 that he was "fine" with legalizing same-sex marriage.

Still, despite the legality of same-sex marriage, many conservative Midwestern and Southern states deny other legal protections to LBGTQ persons. Twenty-nine states still allow licensed professionals to conduct youth gay-conversion therapy, a discredited process to convert LGBTQ people into no longer being queer.

More than 20 states allow discrimination in both housing and public accommodations based on sexual orientation.

Respect for Marriage

Sens. Mitt Romney of Utah, Susan Collins of Maine and Lisa Murkowski, representing Alaska, are among the 12 moderate Republican politicians who voted to advance the same-sex marriage bill.

"I have long supported marriage equality and believe all lawful marriages deserve respect," Murkowski said in a statement on Nov. 16, 2022. "All Americans deserve dignity, respect and equal protection under the law."

Some Republican leaders, though, have grown bolder in their opposition to same-sex marriage since the Supreme Court overturned the constitutional right to abortion in the *Dobbs v. Jackson Women's Health Organization* decision.

These Republicans have said that codifying federal law same-sex marriage is not necessary since they don't believe the Supreme Court is likely to overturn federal protections for same-sex marriage.

Democrats first moved to protect same-sex marriage in federal law because Supreme Court Justice Clarence Thomas wrote in a concurring opinion in the Dobbs case that the court should reconsider, "all of this Court's substantive due process precedents, including Griswold, Lawrence, and Obergefell," the latter being the case that legalized same-sex marriage.

But despite public opinion polls showing that most people favor legalizing same-sex marriage—including nearly half of Republicans—the issue could still be a liability for Republican politicians.

Should the Senate approve the bill—it is to hold a final vote by the end of November 2022—Republicans will then have to answer to their core conservative constituents who largely oppose the practice. This could mean that Senate Republicans may have to consider splitting from their own base, or stepping away from moderate voters.

Periodical and Internet Sources Bibliography

The following articles have been selected to supplement the diverse views presented in this chapter.

Richard Arrington, "Transgenderism: Is Restroom Choice All There Is to It?" *American Conservative*, July 5, 2021. https://www.theamericanconservative.com/transgenderism-is-restroom-choice-all-there-is-to-it/.

Michael Gerson, "How the Gay Rights Movement Found Such Stunning Success," *Washington Post*, June 13, 2022. https://www.washingtonpost.com/opinions/2022/06/13/gay-rights-lgbtq-movement-success-reasons.

Emma Green, "America Moved on from its Gay-Rights Movement—and Left a Legal Mess Behind," the *Atlantic*, August 17, 2019. https://www.theatlantic.com/politics/archive/2019/08/lgbtq-rights-america-arent-resolved/596287/.

Emma Green, "Half of Americans Don't Think Transgender People Should Be Able to Pick Their Bathroom," the *Atlantic*, September 28, 2016. https://www.theatlantic.com/politics/archive/2016/09/half-of-americans-dont-think-transgender-people-should-be-able-to-pick-their-bathroom/501947/.

Nate Hochman, "MLB's Unseemly Support for Youth Gender Transitions," *National Review*, August 31, 2022. https://www.nationalreview.com/2022/08/the-mlbs-unseemly-support-for-youth-gender-transitions/.

Ellen McCarthy, "A Generation of LGBTQ Advocates Hopes the Clock Isn't Ticking Backward," *Washington Post*, May 20, 2022. https://www.washingtonpost.com/lifestyle/2022/05/20/lgbtq-progress/.

Ian Millhiser, "The Constitutional Problem with Florida's 'Don't Say Gay Bill,'" Vox, March 15, 2022. https://www.vox.com/2022/3/15/22976868/dont-say-gay-florida-unconstitutional-ron-desantis-supreme-court-first-amendment-schools-parents.

Alyssa Rosenberg, "If 'Lightyear' Can Spark a Backlash, Then No LGBTQ Victories Are Safe," *Washington Post*, June 22, 2022. https://www.washingtonpost.com/opinions/2022/06/22/lightyear-lesbian-kiss-lgbtq-backlash/.

Kate Sosin, "In Some States, Versions of 'Don't Say Gay' Bills Have Been Around for Awhile," PBS NewsHour, April 20, 2022. https://www.pbs.org/newshour/nation/in-some-states-versions-of-dont-say-gay-bills-have-been-around-for-awhile.

Keeanga-Yamahtta Taylor, "Gay Pride Doesn't Mean Gay Liberation," the *Nation*, June 26, 2019. https://www.thenation.com/article/archive/lgbtq-liberation-nigel-shelby-stonewall.

OPPOSING VIEWPOINTS® SERIES

CHAPTER 2

How Do Transgender Rights Affect Participation in Sports?

Chapter Preface

This chapter takes on the surprisingly complex question of whether transgender people, particularly transgender women, should be allowed to compete on sports teams that match their gender. To some, the issue of transgender people in sports may seem trivial. After all, trans people face obstacles to finding jobs, getting adequate health care, finding places to live, and receiving equitable treatment by the criminal justice system. In some cases, their very lives are threatened. But it is not a trivial issue, particularly for transgender youth.

The authors of the viewpoints in this chapter discuss the issue of fairness. Is it fair for trans women to compete with cisgender women in sports? Or do trans women have a competitive advantage? Are trans women stronger, faster, and otherwise advantaged in sports? The discussion often comes down to hormones, with the assumption that male hormones, particularly testosterone, create muscle and provide an advantage to trans athletes over cis athletes. However, one viewpoint author digs deep into the biology of sex, and points out that our normal intuitions about sex and gender aren't always useful. When it comes to the biology of sex and gender, things are much more complicated than they often seem.

The viewpoints in this chapter take into consideration the perspectives of physicians, students, and athletes themselves, both LGBTQIA+ and not. All approach the issue from slightly different angles discussing sports as divergent as Olympic swimming and roller derby. Some argue that transgender women should be allowed to compete with cis women. Some say no: trans women have an unfair advantage. Most argue for more nuanced and carefully thought-out rules regarding hormone status, particularly in relation to puberty. They all agree, however, that this is a very complex issue and developing standards that are fair to everyone is not going to be easy.

VIEWPOINT 1

> "The rules for participating in K-12 sports will be more stringent than those governing the Olympics. What kind of craziness is that? We're talking about two clumps of kids that just want to kick the ball around."

It's Harmful to Ban Trans People from Sports

Wren Sanders

In this viewpoint, Wren Sanders interviews Dr. Vinny Chulani, the director of the Phoenix Children's Hospital Adolescent Medicine Program and expert in the field of LGBTQIA+ care, about laws banning trans youth from sports, particularly Idaho's "Fairness in Women's Sports Act," which was passed and signed into law in 2020 and prevents transgender girls and women from participating in girls' and women's collegiate and K–12 sports. Though it was the first bill of its kind of be passed into law, it is far from the last. Chulani explains the many reasons these laws are harmful. Wren Sanders is a journalist who often writes about LGBTQIA+ issues and is a community editor of Them, *a magazine covering LGBTQIA+ issues.*

As you read, consider the following questions:

1. How does Idaho's "Fairness in Women's Sports Act" stipulate settling disputes over a students' gender?

"A Doctor Explains Why Banning Trans People from Sports Is Wrong," by Wren Sanders, Them, April 9, 2020. Reprinted by permission.

2. According to this viewpoint, what made some people think the "Fairness in Women's Sports Act" was less about fairness and more about attacking rights of trans people?
3. According to Dr. Chulani, why does it damage trans people to ban them from changing their gender on their birth certificates?

On March 30, Idaho's Republican governor Brad Little signed the "Fairness in Women's Sports Act" into law, a bill that bans trans and intersex girls from competing in women's athletics at the youth, high school, and college levels. The legislation, passed the day after International Transgender Day of Visibility, states that "athletic teams or sports designated for females, women, or girls shall not be open to students of the male sex," and specifies that a "dispute" about an athlete's gender can only be resolved through a physician's examination of "the student's reproductive anatomy, genetic makeup, or normal endogenously produced testosterone levels." Of at least nine other states actively considering similar bans on trans women's participation in women's sports, Idaho is the first to pass one into law.

Critics were quick to point out the cruelty of the bill's timing, passed when all gatherings—let alone athletic events—had been cancelled or postponed to stop the spread of the coronavirus. And as Vox reported, there were no openly trans athletes participating in youth or college-level sports in Idaho when the bill passed, either. Coupled with the fact that Governor Little signed legislation barring Idahoans from changing the gender marker on birth certificates on the same day, many saw Idaho's "Fairness in Women's Sports Act" as less about "fairness" and more about brazenly attacking the rights of trans people.

These bills promise to hold dire consequences for trans people in the state and in all parts of the country where similar legislation is being pursued. To learn more about the debate surrounding trans participation in women's sports and the danger posed by bills that prevent it, we spoke to Dr. Vinny Chulani, Director of the Phoenix Children's Hospital Adolescent Medicine Program, an esteemed practitioner in the field of LGBTQ+ care and an ardent advocate of the rights of trans and gender-nonconforming youth. Below, Dr. Chulani outlines the grave mental health implications Idaho's bill will wreak, and the medical and scientific misunderstandings that inform such legislation in the first place.

Q: What was your initial reaction to hearing about that bill, particularly the one that was designed to prohibit trans women from competing in women's sports?

A: I was especially surprised to see the bill go through the Idaho legislature because at the same time that this was happening, we had a very similar house bill here in Arizona, House Bill 2706, which was entitled "Save Women In Sports Act." What's especially draconian about what's going on in Idaho is that they have an additional piece of legislation that bars people from changing their gender marker on their birth certificate. This will be especially harmful because birth certificates are often a person's primary proof of citizenship. They open doors to a wide range of services. This decision is really unfortunate.

Q: What do you see as the main negative consequences of this kind of legislation?

A: First, there are the implications of this bill on the social and emotional well being of TGNC youth. We have a tremendous body of literature that talks about the benefits of sports participation on confidence and character building, on competence, on coping; there's so much that sport can offer. And we also know that there's a tremendous disparity in the rates of anxiety and depression and suicide among TGNC youth versus their cisgender peers. If anything, we should work to eliminate these disparities by encouraging and engaging all young people in sports. Where 68%

Fifty-five Percent of Americans Oppose Letting Transgender Girls and Women Compete

A new poll conducted by *The Washington Post* and University of Maryland found the majority of Americans, 55 percent, are opposed to allowing transgender female athletes to compete with other women and girls in high school sports. A higher proportion, 58 percent, reported the same opinion at the college and professional sports levels.

A total of 1,503 adults completed the poll between May 4 and 17, 2022, representing a random sample of U.S. households. The majority of individuals surveyed identified themselves as sports fans and were parents.

While 15 percent of respondents had no opinion on the matter, around 30 percent of Americans agree transgender women and girl athletes should be able to compete at any sporting level.

When it comes to youth sports, differences in opinion were slightly less pronounced, with 49 percent of those surveyed opposed to transgender athletes' participation, 33 percent in favor and 17 percent reporting no opinion.

Nearly 70 percent of respondents said they believed transgender girls would have a competitive advantage over other girls, with 30 percent reporting neither group would have an advantage.

However, a slim majority of those surveyed did say they were concerned with transgender athletes' mental health in the event they were not allowed to participate in youth sports.

The notion of supporting transgender people along their journey yet having reservations when it comes to athletic competition is common, said Mark Hyman, director of UMD's Shirley Povich Center for Sports Journalism which also helped conduct the poll.

"People increasingly have an awareness of the issue and are empathetic toward the journey that transgender people are on, but the notion that they are competing against athletes that are born a particular sex are lagging behind that," Hyman told *The Washington Post*.

How Do Transgender Rights Affect Participation in Sports?

> According to new data released this month by the UCLA Williams Institute, 43 percent of those who identify as transgender in the U.S. are teens and young adults.
>
> Previous research has also showed those who have a transgender family member or friend are more likely to support greater acceptance of the transgender community and feel this is good for society.
>
> This sentiment is sharply split along party lines as 64 percent of Democrats feel greater social acceptance of transgender individuals is good for society, compared with just 14 percent of Republicans.
>
> "New Poll Finds Majority of Americans Against Trans Athletes in Female Sports," by Gianna Melillo, The Hill, June 14, 2022.

of cisgender students are involved in sports, only around 10 to 15% of our transgender youth are, too. This bill creates an additional layer of stigma and therefore deprives young people of the benefits of being able to participate in sports.

The second thing that I think is really an area of concern for me is how this is a decision that is really not based on science. There are so many characteristics that contribute to excellence in sports. And the same attributes don't always carry over from one sport to the next. You need different skills for golfing than you need for archery, basketball, soccer, or gymnastics. Plus, there's not really any sound body of evidence that speaks to the advantage that testosterone confers. When you take a look at some of the studies that have been done on transgender females in terms of their athletic ability, it overlaps with the range that you would find in cisgender women. There is no body of evidence to suggest that there is an advantage.

The third thing that's really problematic about the law is its implementation, which promises to force women to prove their womanhood... This puts the burden of proof on the accused. Now some might have to submit to a blood test at [their] expense. What does this mean for people that can't afford karyotyping or don't have access to medical care? The other thing that's crazy about this is that it's being applied to kids in K-12. That means the rules for participating in K-12 sports will be more stringent than those governing the Olympics. What kind of craziness is that? We're talking about two clumps of kids that just want to kick the ball around.

Q: You suggested that this kind of legislation is not based on science, but rather opportunistic readings of existing studies. What do those who support preventing trans women's participation in women's sports misunderstand most about sex, bodies, and gender?

A: That these are fixed processes and that transgender women are really men who are homogeneous in terms of their strength and are uniformly stronger than any woman. Bills like Idaho's fail to recognize the diversity within the transgender female population. They also fail to understand the biology of puberty and where we are presently in terms of treatment, specifically with puberty blockers. Remember that when you take a look at pre-pubertal bodies, assigned male and assigned female bodies look a lot alike; it's not until puberty that they go their different ways under the influence of sex steroids… Nowadays, if you have a patient in early puberty who was assigned male at birth and has gender distress or gender questions, we can use puberty blockers to suppress male puberty. They would not develop the traits that would theoretically afford them the advantage. Yet this child, under Idaho law, would still be excluded.

These bills are coded in the language of fairness. And yet they are being considered and passed at a time when organized sports are not happening. Given that knowledge, do you believe fairness is what is being protected here, or potentially something else?

This law in Idaho has to be viewed in the context of the march that we are seeing in legislative houses across the country. Let's not be ignorant, right? This is part of a larger anti-transgender agenda. Let's not deceive ourselves that it's anything other than that.

Q: Considering the broader anti-trans agenda, what worries you most as bills like the recently passed ones in Idaho continue moving through state legislatures?

A: How they harm young people through enforcing already existing stigma. Young trans people may choose to not participate in sports. But even if they might not want to participate in sports, at least that option should be there for them. It's tough enough.

The opinions expressed in this interview, which has been edited and condensed for clarity, are Dr. Chulani's own, and do not reflect those of any organization of which he is a part, including the Phoenix Children's hospital.

VIEWPOINT 2

> "If the NCAA really wanted equality for their trans athletes, they would be holding them by the same regulations that the biological women are held to."

The NCAA Should Change Its Regulations Regarding Trans Athletes
Evan Mills

In this viewpoint, student journalist Evan Mills explains the controversy surrounding swimmer Lia Thomas, a trans woman who is a college swimmer, and offers a solution to the problem of deciding when and how trans women can compete in women's sporting events. Since trans women who have been taking hormone blockers for one year still have higher levels of testosterone than the designated limit for cisgender female athletes, Mills suggests that trans athletes should be required to take hormone blockers for over two years to ensure fairness. At the time this viewpoint was published, Mills was a staff writer for the Herd, the online newspaper and magazine of Kennebunk High School, Kennebunk, Maine.

As you read, consider the following questions:

1. What physical advantages does Thomas have over other female competitors, according to this viewpoint?

"Should Transgender Athletes Be Allowed to Compete in Sports?" by Evan Mills, March 29, 2022. Reprinted by permission.

2. What is Title IX, and according to Mills, how does it relate to the issue of trans women in sports?
3. How does Mills suggest resolving the situation?

With the recent controversial NCAA Swimming National Championships taking place, the national attention exploded with discussion. Now, you may be wondering why people are actually paying attention to college swimming on a national level, but it is because a transgender woman name Lia Thomas ended up winning the 500m race. An eruption of public outrage spewed after the race and many people didn't like that the NCAA allowed a biological man to compete against biological women and saw a massive physical advantage for Thomas. The NCAA later came out and said that it was in support of Lia's win and for any other transgender athlete's participation in college athletics in the name of inclusivity and being anti-transphobic. Even many other women swimmers were against it with letters from 36 Arizona women's alumni swimmers; Texas women's alumni swimmers; and even some of Thomas's own teammates expressing their concerns to the NCAA about allowing her to compete in races against biological women. So, is there really an advantage for Lia Thomas and transgender women in sports?

To start out, Lia Thomas absolutely had an advantage over the other competitors in terms of physical stature. What I mean by this is that Lia went through puberty as a boy and completed puberty as a man while the other swimmers started puberty as girls and finished as women. The biological differences between the sexes are one of the main reasons that many say she had an advantage over the other swimmers. Men develop broader shoulders during puberty which is extremely important in swimming so you can pull through the water at a faster rate and with less water resistance. Men generally develop larger hands and feet which are important because the larger surface area covered by your feet and hands, the more water you pull and the faster you will go. Also, since men generally tend to be taller than women after puberty, larger lungs are developed which help with increased endurance and buoyancy (the ability to float), which is important for long distance swimmers and also for swimmers to stay above the water during a race. Lastly, men have a much higher amount of natural testosterone than women do even after taking hormone blockers for a full year like Thomas has. The increased amounts of testosterone lead to higher muscle mass, bone density and also the amount of hemoglobin in the body. Hemoglobin is a protein in red blood cells that carry oxygen to different parts of the body. So, if you have more testosterone and hemoglobin, you have a higher rate of endurance.

Next, it is important to look at the biological advantages that transgender women have compared to cisgender women even while taking hormone blockers. The NCAA restrictions are set to where a transgender female athlete must take hormone blockers for a full year before being able to compete, as well as a testosterone level of 10 nmol/L or lower. The NCAA, however, only allows cisgender women to have a maximum of 5 nmol/L or less of testosterone which is proof that there is a visible advantage for transgender athletes in the NCAA. A study done by Dr. Timothy Roberts, a pediatrician from Children's Mercy Hospital in Kansas City, shows that transgender women after two years of hormone blockers retain a 12% advantage against their cisgender counterparts in terms of overall speed in a 1.5 mile run; a 10% higher number in terms of pushups done; and a 6% difference in the amount of situps that were done. This study was based on a physical test done every 6-12 months by the U.S. Airforce and tested a pool of 46 transgender women. Another reason testosterone is so important in this issue is because it also shows how the discrepancies between cis men and trans men were closed after two years of taking testosterone. Before taking testosterone, the trans men had significantly lower amounts of pushups and situps, as well as much slower 1.5 mile times. This fact goes a long way to show why transgender women athletes should be held to the same requirements as cisgender women based on testosterone levels. Another study done by Tommy Lundberg, a research scientist at Sweden's Karolinska Institute, found that transgender women getting feminizing hormone therapy after one year still had significant advantages in terms of muscular strength and bone strength "to the point that fairness cannot be ensured in most sports," according to Lundburg. Now, there still haven't been many studies on this issue which is why it is still such a heated debate topic, but from what has been studied, it seems like trans women still will have higher testosterone levels even while on hormone blockers compared to cisgender women.

Finally, if the NCAA really wanted equality for their trans athletes, they would be holding them by the same regulations that the biological women are held to. Female athletes fought tirelessly for Title IX to be instituted by the Supreme Court and this seems like it could possibly lead to the downfall of women's sports from issues like these. If there is going to be a continual rise of this happening, biological men will start to dominate women's sports and we could have a whole other set of issues that come along with it. The best way to stop all of the controversy from this is for the NCAA to hold trans athletes to the same levels of hormones as cis athletes and also extend the amount of time that is required to be on hormone blockers to over two years to get rid of any extreme physical discrepancy.

To end this off, it is not the trans athletes' faults for the issues at hand. It is purely the people at the top of the NCAA board for causing this to be an issue because they allow for these advantages to occur while other boards like the IOC have done their research and have been able to have more equitable athletic events. A few, simple regulation changes could possibly put this issue to a close. It is not a matter of anti-inclusivity of trans athletes, it is a matter of equality between transgender and cis gender women in sports.

VIEWPOINT 3

> "As an Olympic champion and as a civil rights lawyer, I can assure you that there was nothing fair about transgender woman Lia Thomas competing for the University of Pennsylvania in NCAA swimming."

Transgender Women Should Compete, but Only If They've Mitigated the Advantages of Male Puberty

Nancy Hogshead-Makar

In this viewpoint, a guest editorial in the magazine Swimming World, *Hogshead-Makar responds to the Lia Thomas controversy. She argues that Thomas's case is different from that of other trans women athletes because Thomas went through male puberty. After one year of hormone suppression treatment, she was only 2.6 percent slower than she has been before transitioning in the 200-yard freestyle and 5.76 percent slower in the 500-yard freestyle, which does not compensate for the 11 percent advantage in swimming times that male athletes have. Nancy Hogshead-Makar is an Olympic medalist in swimming and advocate for girls and women in sport.*

"Sex Matters: Why Transgender Athletes Must Not Compete Against Biological Females," Swimming World, February 12, 2022. Reprinted by permission.

How Do Transgender Rights Affect Participation in Sports?

As you read, consider the following questions:

1. How does Hogshead-Makar compare Lia Thomas to the East German swim team?
2. In what way did Title IX help Hogshead-Makar, according to this viewpoint?
3. What data is used here to back up the argument that Thomas is not competing fairly as a woman?

Nancy Hogshead-Makar knows all about being a champion in the pool, and championing for the rights of female athletes. A four-time medalist at the 1984 Olympic Games in Los Angeles, Hogshead-Makar has long fought for equality in women's sports and is the head of Champion Women, which advocates for girls and women in sports. Hogshead-Makar wrote the following editorial in response to the controversy surrounding transgender swimmer Lia Thomas.

Inclusion and fairness are two vital values in the world of sports.

Transgender women should be allowed to compete in women's athletics, so long as these individuals can show that they've mitigated the athletic advantages that come with male puberty.

As an Olympic champion and as a civil rights lawyer, I can assure you that there was nothing fair about transgender woman Lia Thomas competing for the University of Pennsylvania in NCAA swimming.

Worse, her domination of the "women's sports" category has done nothing to engender greater empathy for inclusive practices throughout society for the trans community.

I swam on the U.S. National Team for nine years, from 1976–1984, the same years that East German swimmers dominated women's competitions by cheating with anabolic steroids.

I was able to win three Olympic gold medals and a silver medal because the East Germans boycotted the 1984 Los Angeles Olympic Games.

We all knew they were cheating. The boycott announcement was a relief; I knew I'd have a fair shot at winning.

My Olympic gold medals changed the trajectory of my life.

Title IX, the federal law that prohibits sex discrimination, permits sex-segregation in sport—which means that, for the most part, men compete against men, and women compete against women.

Title IX gave me a fair opportunity to win and set records, as well as access to money, accolades, and leadership opportunities.

If Congress and courts had forbidden sex-segregated sports, the way race and religious segregation is prohibited, I would have qualified for my high school team, but I'd never have been the Hall of Famer that I became.

I doubt I'd have competed past high school.

Now imagine if all schools were only responsible for sponsoring one sports team and they put their best students—regardless of gender—on that team.

How many girls and women would make it?

For sure, millions of girls and women would lose out on the educational experience that participation in sports provides. An experience which is also linked to economic success and life-long health.

Trans women should compete with biological women, so long as they can demonstrate that they have lost their sex-linked, male-puberty advantage prior to competition in the women's category.

Lia Thomas cannot make that demonstration.

While she has apparently been complying with NCAA rules requiring hormone therapy for over 2 ½ years now, she still competes with an unfair advantage.

How do we know Lia Thomas' performances aren't fair?

The average differential in the men's and women's 'A' standard times for NCAA championship qualification is 11.41%; meaning the women's times are 11%+ slower than the men's qualification times.

About the same differential occurs if you're looking at almost any group of swimming records or qualification times between men and women, including regional or USA Swimming qualification times, American records, world records, NCAA records.

The gaps between men and women are generally larger in the sprints than they are in the long-distance events.

So, how big is that 11% advantage in swimming times for male swimmers?

Enormous.

To put it in perspective, Olympic superstar Michael Phelps held just a .08% of an advantage over his U.S. teammate and rival Ian Crocker in the 100 butterfly in the 2004 Olympics.

But Phelps held a 12.62% advantage over the women's gold medalist, Australian Petria Thomas.

Phelps' advantage over women equates to over 150 times more than the advantage that Phelps had over his male competitors.

If he had that same 12.62% advantage over his male competitors, he would have swam 6.47 seconds faster than he did to win the gold, or a time of 44.78 seconds.

Meanwhile, the gap between first and eighth in the men's Olympic final was a tiny gap of just 1.31 seconds.

Lia Thomas, however, was not 11% slower. She was only 2.6% slower than she was pre-transition in the 200-yard freestyle, and just 5.76% slower in the 500-yard freestyle.

That is NOT mitigation. It is NOT fair.

I should add that it isn't Lia's fault.

The problem is with the NCAA's rules that permitted Penn to keep her on their women's team.

(Prior to the NCAA passing its transgender determination rules to USA Swimming, the governing body for college sports followed this rule).

"A trans female treated with testosterone suppression medication may continue to compete on the men's team but may not compete on the women's team without changing it to a mixed team status until completing one year of testosterone suppression treatment."

But "one year of testosterone suppression treatment" was not sufficient to level the playing field between Thomas and her female competitors.

If seven-time U.S. Olympic champion Caeleb Dressel transitioned and was somehow able to mitigate the advantage he gained during male puberty, including any legacy advantage, and then broke women's swimming events, I'd think this outcome was fair.

Dressel is, after all, a once-in-a-generation athlete.

Thomas was never in that category of standout athlete for the many years she competed as a male.

Thomas proved that the advocates who assured the NCAA and their member schools that male puberty could be rolled back in a single year after consistent hormone treatment were wrong.

The rules should follow the evidence, and in this case it is clear: Thomas should not have been in head-to-head competition with biological females.

2020 research on transgender women athletes by Emma Hilton and Tommy Lundberg concluded that: "The biological advantage, most notably in terms of muscle mass and strength, conferred by male puberty and thus enjoyed by most transgender women is only minimally reduced when testosterone is suppressed as per current sporting guidelines for transgender athletes."

Thomas qualified and could have competed in the men's category, or could have competed in an exhibition race (where her results would not count) until the evidence and science catches up with sports practices.

In all my years competing with East German women who were doped to the gills, they were only slightly better than the best biological women; not one of them were competitive with men.

Moreover, if I had tested positive for testosterone, I probably would have suffered a four-year suspension from international competition.

But if I tested positive twice? I'd be banned for life.

Because the World Anti-Doping (Agency) knows that long-term testosterone use produces legacy effects that last much longer than just during the time it is used.

Critics of mine will likely ask: what about the goals of transgender inclusion in sport?

We know that transgender students are subject to bullying and high rates of suicide.

The argument is that girls and women should step aside and make way for transgender athletes to compete in the "girls' and women's" sports categories, considering the blatant discrimination they face.

I say—no.

Transgender Female Athletes Do Not Necessarily Have a Physical Advantage

The conversation into whether transgender athletes have an unfair advantage over female competitors has reignited this week after Gov. Ron DeSantis issued a proclamation declaring Sarasota native Emma Weyant the real winner of a NCAA swim meet in the 500-yard freestyle event.

During the competition, Weyant was defeated by Lia Thomas, a transgender athlete who underwent gender reassignment surgery in 2019.

Thomas defeated Weyant, an Olympic silver medalist, by more than one second. Yet, if she had the same time during the 2019 race, she would have placed third.

Thomas placed fifth and eighth in her other two races at the competition.

Though the overall competition saw 27 all-time NCAA records broken, Thomas didn't break any of them. Thomas' win trails Olympic swimmer Katie Ledecky's 2017 record by about nine seconds. That's a lot of time in swimming.

continued on next page

> Dr. Maureen Whelihan performs hormone therapy for transgender patients in South Florida. She said each case is unique.
>
> "I think it would be a case-by-case situation based on how long did you spend as a male before you became female," said Whelihan. "How much muscle mass did you develop as a male before you became female? So, it really wouldn't be cut and dry. You need to have some formula to begin with."
>
> Whelihan said a large determining factor could be when the patient underwent gender reassignment surgery and what is the history of the patient pre-surgery.
>
> "You really have to separate the patients or the individuals by how developed they've gotten as individual in the "X-Y" before they started transitioning to a woman and, boy, that would be a lot to sort through, because there are such variations in that," said Whelihan.
>
> Whelihan said patients can retain muscle mass up to four years post gender surgery. However, without normal male testosterone production, those muscles would not sustain the same amount of strength.
>
> Last year, DeSantis signed a bill banning transgender athletes from competing in female sports at the high school and collegiate levels, making females' eligibility to compete in female sports based on their biological sex given at birth.
>
> "Do Transgender Athletes Really Have an Unfair Advantage?" by Derek Lowe, WPTV, March 24, 2022.

Girls and women shouldn't give up their hard-won sports opportunities, no matter how real the harms suffered by transgender athletes.

Allowing transgender women to change the meaning of the women's category makes as much sense as allowing 180-pound athletes into the 120-pound weight category, because larger athletes were subject to awful bullying and harassment.

Or allowing adults to compete against children, or only permitting impoverished nations compete in the Olympics.

Sport has been set up as binary with males and females, and sport needs to adapt by adding new events and classifications,

How Do Transgender Rights Affect Participation in Sports?

rather than throwing out the meaning of the "girls' and women's" categories.

Rather than trying to squeeze transgender athletes into one-of-two categories, male or female, sport needs to adapt.

I've now been an advocate for Title IX, the federal law requiring schools to prohibit sex discrimination, since the 1984 Olympics when I won my medals.

As a civil rights lawyer, I run Champion Women, a non-profit that provides legal advocacy for girls and women in sports. We produce data—for athletes, families, alumni and donors—which demonstrates just how badly 90% of colleges and universities are discriminating against women.

In total, women are denied over 183,000 opportunities to play collegiate sports, they're denied over a billion dollars in athletic scholarships, and hundreds and millions of dollars in treatment, meaning women aren't being given equal facilities, locker rooms, medical care, publicity, travel, and so forth.

I've never met a single female athlete that couldn't list the ways they're getting second-class treatment as compared to their male football or basketball players.

In those 38 years, I've never heard a single man say, "Oh you women face such overwhelming sex discrimination throughout society, particularly in sexual harassment and violence. Here, take our athletic facilities and scholarships."

Quite the opposite.

The unwritten rule is that women's sports can exist, so long as not a single male is harmed by women's inclusion.

And yet, notice that women are expected to graciously move over and let trans athlete-inclusion change the meaning of the "women's sports" category.

It is sexist; we'd never allow the meaning of NCAA "men's sports" category to change so that current NFL and NBA teams could be included.

We'd never allow 25-year-old men to compete in boy's high school events. And we would never tell those boys to just "work harder" if they wanted to win.

I am ready to hear men's outrage. I am ready for men to step up and make sports equality happen for women's sports.

Lia Thomas showed all of us that the current rules are not fair and forcing her into the women's category only engenders resentment.

That doesn't mean, however, that transgender athletes should be excluded from the many benefits of sport.

Instead, sport must adapt in creative ways that are not harmful to the women's category.

VIEWPOINT 4

> *"On the whole, the physical differences among men and among women are bigger than the differences between men and women."*

We Need Better Solutions for Gender-Segregated Sports

Katharina Lindner

The two previous viewpoints considered the question of whether transgender athletes have an unfair advantage in sport. Here, Katharina Lindner looks at the same question, but takes a much closer look at the biology. Nature, she says, "is messier than we think," making decisions around transgender athletes far more complicated than many make them out to be. Because hormone levels differ widely both among men and among women, determining an "acceptable" hormone level for someone of either sex is pretty arbitrary. Katharina Linder was a lecturer and member of the Centre for Gender and Feminist Studies at the University of Stirling in the United Kingdom. She is also a former professional soccer player.

As you read, consider the following questions:

1. How do the requirements for trans women to compete differ from those for men? Why do they differ?

"Do Transgender Athletes Have an Unfair Advantage?" by Katharina Lindner, The Conversation, February 9, 2016. https://theconversation.com/do-transgender-athletes-have-an-unfair-advantage-54289. Licensed under CC BY 4.0 International.

2. Other writers in this chapter have suggested that hormone levels are the best way of determining whether an athlete should compete as a woman or as a man. Lindner says this is "arbitrary" and "useless." What is her reasoning?
3. According to Lindner, in what way is the biology of sex complicated?

It hasn't always been plain sailing for women in sport. With a history marked by division and discrimination, it looks like things could be about to get a whole lot more complicated for female athletes, after the International Olympic Committee announced changes to its transgender policy.

Transgender athletes will now be allowed to compete in the Olympics without having to undergo sex reassignment surgery. Which is possibly set to impact women's sport more than men's. Achieving eligibility to compete in male competition is now easy—you just have to say you are male. Whereas eligibility to compete in female competition is subject to a number of tests for hormone levels.

For some, this step away from surgical requirements was enthusiastically welcomed and considered an important milestone towards greater equality and inclusion in the sporting world. But there were also much more critical responses. These included concerns around the possible impact on the integrity and fairness of competition. And fears that women in particular would be even further disadvantaged within sport than they already are.

Questions of Biology

The *Times* columnist Janice Turner said the new policy was "great news—unless you are a woman athlete" and that "trans athletes are unfair to women". Her concerns are based on assumptions that male-to-female trans athletes will always have a biological advantage in terms of size, muscle mass and lung capacity.

For Turner, the new policy, while seemingly more inclusive, is bound to be exploited by "medal-hungry male athletes in unscrupulous nations." One example Turner mentions is the case of the Iranian women's football national team, which allegedly includes eight men who are currently "awaiting sex change operations".

But female athletes, especially the most talented ones have long had their gender called into question. In 2009 Caster Semenya the female South-African middle distance runner, was forced to undergo sex testing after her 800-metre victory at the 2009 World Championships was considered too fast for a woman. Which is another example that demonstrates how debates about unfair competitive advantage intersect with concerns around "real" female athletes' marginalisation.

Testing Time

The move towards using hormone levels for purposes of sex testing and in transgender inclusion policies is useful. It is hormones, especially androgens such as testosterone—and not reproductive organs—that are linked to muscle mass, speed and strength and competitive advantage.

But here's where the trouble starts. The "female" sex hormone oestrogen is generally found in higher levels in women. And men tend to have higher levels of androgens like testosterone. But both oestrogens and androgens are also found in men and women. Making any cutoff point, such as trans women requiring a consistent testosterone level below 10 nmol/L—the level set by the IOC—is pretty arbitrary, and ultimately useless.

The IOC's use of hormone levels to measure or test sex has replaced earlier "gender verification" practices. These previously involved asking female athletes to drop their underwear, but eventually a less humiliating method was found: checking swabs of cheek tissue for chromosomes, as "proof" of an athlete's sex. Women have vaginas, ovaries and XX chromosomes, and men have penises and XY chromosomes. Sounds simple right? Wrong.

The move away from using reproductive organs or chromosomes was linked to scientific evidence which showed that "nature" is a lot messier than we think. There is no neat and clear distinction between "male" and "female"—and no way of "measuring" or "testing" sex based on reproductive organs or chromosomes alone.

There are much greater variations of sex chromosomes than simply XX and XY, including XXY, XXXY, XXXXY, XXYY, XXXYY. And chromosomes themselves also don't have a direct impact on the body's physical characteristics—they only do so when combined with certain hormones. Then add intersex people, discrepancies between internal and external sex organs and mismatches between genitals and chromosomal sex into the mix - and you've got a whole lot of complication. As was the case with Semenya.

Facing the Future

On the whole, the physical differences among men and among women are bigger than the differences between men and women. Semenya might have higher testosterone levels and greater muscles mass than the "average woman"—but the same might also be said about Usain Bolt when compared to the "average man."

The IOC's new policy is then, perhaps, the best we can do, at the moment, given that sport is a gender-segregated context.

Removing the need for transgender athletes to undergo sex reassignment surgery is a welcome acknowledgement that bodies don't come in neatly defined categories. And using hormone levels as a measure seems a pragmatic compromise. That said, the increasingly popular sport of roller derby puts the rest of the sporting world to shame with its move away from gender-segregation and its refreshingly progressive policies for trans people, genderqueer and nonbinary inclusion.

Assuming mainstream sport will remain gender-segregated for the time being, what is needed then is education to prevent prejudice, exclusion and knee-jerk reactions by sports policy makers, governing bodies and the media. And continuing conversations between those promoting equality for women in sport and advocates for transgender inclusion are vital to iron out any unproductive misconceptions on both sides.

VIEWPOINT 5

> *"Since studies have shown that kids who participate meaningfully in athletics have better mental and physical health than their peers who don't—and teens who identify as transgender are at a significantly greater mental health risk than their peers—it's a worthy goal to try to accommodate their desire to compete."*

A Balance Must Be Struck Between Fairness in Sports and Transgender Rights

Chris W. Surprenant

In this viewpoint, Chris W. Surprenant explains why the issue of transgender girls and women competing in sports is such a fraught one. He explains that this is because despite the fact that the number of transgender athletes is low—especially at the high school level—a handful of trans athletes have been very successful, which has caused politicians and political activists to latch onto the examples and push legislation that would ban all trans athletes from participating. However, Surprenant argues that studies indicate that children and teens experience considerable mental and physical health benefits from meaningfully participating in sports, and trans athletes should

"Striking a Balance Between Fairness in Competition and the Rights of Transgender Athletes," by Chris W. Surprenant, The Conversation, May 18, 2021. https://theconversation.com/striking-a-balance-between-fairness-in-competition-and-the-rights-of-transgender-athletes-159685. Licensed under CC BY 4.0 International..

not be categorically denied these benefits. Chris W. Surprenant is a professor of ethics, strategy, and public policy at the University of New Orleans.

As you read, consider the following questions:

1. What does Surprenant mean by allowing someone to "participate meaningfully" in sports?
2. According to data cited in the viewpoint, how has Title IX impacted athletic participation for women and girls?
3. How does Surprenant suggest balancing fairness and inclusiveness for transgender athletes?

In a majority of U.S. states, bills aiming to restrict who can compete in women's sports at public institutions have either been signed into law or are working their way through state legislatures.

Caught up in this political point-scoring are real people—both trans athletes who want to participate in competitive sports and those competing against them.

As a professor of ethics and public policy, I spend much of my time thinking about the role of the law in protecting the rights of individuals, especially when the rights of some people appear to conflict with the rights of others.

How to accommodate transgender athletes in competitive sports—or whether they should be accommodated at all—has become one of these conflicts.

On one side are transgender athletes who want to compete in the gender division with which they identify. On the other are political activists and athletes—especially biologically female athletes—who believe that allowing trans athletes to compete in women's divisions is inherently unfair.

So why is this issue so fraught? What's so special about women's sports? Why do women's divisions even exist? And is it possible to

How Do Transgender Rights Affect Participation in Sports?

protect women's sports while still finding a way to allow transgender athletes to compete in a meaningful way?

Winners Elicit Outcry

Let's be clear: Few Americans would care about how to best accommodate transgender athletes if they were not winning events.

But that's exactly what has happened. In 2017 and 2018, Terry Miller, a trans woman, won the Connecticut women's high school track championships in the 55-meter, 100-meter, 200-meter and 300-meter events. Her closest and only real competitor those two years was Andraya Yearwood, who is also a trans woman.

In 2017 and 2018, Mack Beggs, a trans man, dominated the Texas 6A 110-pound girls wrestling division, capturing two state championships while compiling a record of 89 wins and 0 losses. Unlike in Connecticut, where athletes may compete as they identify, athletes in Texas must compete in the gender listed on their birth certificate.

While Miller, Yearwood, Beggs and others have triumphed in their respective sports, the number of transgender high school athletes is very low. Nor is there any evidence that athletes have transitioned for the purpose of gaining a competitive advantage.

Yet some legislators have latched onto these examples, using them as a basis for bills that ban all transgender teens from participating in gendered divisions that differ from their birth sex. But these bills don't solve the competitive imbalances that can occur with athletes like Beggs. Worse, they might prevent transgender teens from competing altogether.

Sports Matter—with Meaningful Participation

Since studies have shown that kids who participate meaningfully in athletics have better mental and physical health than their peers who don't—and teens who identify as transgender are at a significantly greater mental health risk than their peers—it's a worthy goal to try to accommodate their desire to compete.

The phrase "participate meaningfully" is important. Someone who, for example, is nominally on a team but does not take the sport seriously does not participate meaningfully in competitive sports. Similarly, someone who takes a sport seriously but easily dominates all competition also does not participate meaningfully in competition.

Youth sports organizations exist because we don't believe kids should compete against adults, and kids are further separated by age because age, for children, is a reasonably good proxy for skill and ability. Organizations like the Special Olympics and Paralympics exist to provide opportunities for people with physical and mental disabilities to participate meaningfully and compete against people with similar skill sets.

Male and female athletes are separated for the same reason.

The Rise of Women's Sports

In 1972, the U.S. Congress extended Title IX of the Educational Amendments to the 1964 Civil Rights Act to prohibit discrimination in all federally funded education programs, including their associated athletics programs.

Title IX's impact on athletics for women and girls—and, as a result, U.S. culture—has been nothing short of dramatic. In 1970, fewer than 5% of U.S. girls participated in high school sports. Now 43% of high school girls participate in competitive sports.

Separating athletes by biological sex is necessary because the gap between the best male and female athletes—at all levels—is dramatic.

Serena Williams is not only one of the best female tennis players in history, she's one of the best female athletes in history. In 1998, both Serena and her sister Venus famously claimed that no male ranked outside of the ATP Top 200 could beat them. Karsten Braasch, the 203rd-ranked player ATP player at the time, challenged each to a set. Braasch beat Serena 6-1 and Venus 6-2.

"I didn't know it would be that difficult," Serena said after the match. "I played shots that would have been winners on the women's circuit, and he got to them very easily."

At the 2019 New Balance Nationals Outdoor, the national track championship for U.S. high school students, Joseph Fahnbulleh of Minnesota won the men's 100-meter with a time of 10.35 seconds. That same year, Olympic Gold Medal winner Shelly-Ann Fraser-Pryce ran the fastest 100-meter time of any female in the world—10.71 seconds. Her time would have tied for 19th at that U.S. boys high school event.

One more example that's a bit different: In 2012, Keeling Pilaro, a 4-foot-8, 80-pound seventh grade boy, petitioned the New York State Public High School Athletic Association to play field hockey on his school's all-female team. It approved his petition.

As a seventh grader, Pilaro made the school's JV team. As an eighth grader, he made the varsity team. But players and coaches from other schools argued he had a significant advantage because he was a boy. During the summer before his ninth grade year, the league agreed. It ruled Pilaro could no longer participate because his "advanced field hockey skills" had "adversely affected the opportunities of females."

I point to these examples because, put together, they show that no fitness regimen, no amount of practice, and no reallocation of financial resources could allow the best female athletes at any level to compete against the best male athletes at that same level.

This advantage isn't simply a difference in degree—it's not just that male athletes are bigger, faster and stronger—but it's a difference in kind. Pound for pound, male bodies are more athletic.

Evaluating Trans Athletes on a Case-by-Case Basis

So, how can we allow trans athletes to compete without giving them an unfair advantage over their competitors?

One proposed solution, as if taken from the pages of novelist Kurt Vonnegut's "Harrison Bergeron," is testosterone-based handicapping for events. Competitors would have their testosterone levels measured and then algorithms would determine their advantage. Then, competitors would be fitted with weighted clothes, compete on a different track or otherwise receive an appropriate handicap before competing.

But having a higher level of testosterone does not automatically make you a better athlete. Beyond this, while handicapping may be fine for a golf outing with friends, it isn't appropriate for serious athletic contests. The point of athletic competitions is to determine who is actually the best, not who is the best relative to handicaps.

Another proposed solution entails replacing gender divisions entirely with ability-level divisions. Yet this could hinder women's participation in sports. In a world with no female-only divisions, Serena Williams would still win some tennis tournaments, but they likely wouldn't be tournaments you've heard of.

So what's the most viable solution to this debate?

Since there is no typical transgender athlete, broad rules for transgender athletes don't seem appropriate.

Instead, language similar to the Equal Employment Opportunity Commission's disability accommodation policy could be used for transgender athletes: "The decision as to the appropriate accommodation must be based on the particular facts of each case."

"Men's" divisions could be eliminated and replaced with "open" divisions. Any athlete could be allowed to compete in that division.

Then, transgender athletes could be evaluated on a case-by-case basis. Based on their athletic ability, a tournament organizer could determine which division is most fair for them to compete in, "women's" or "open."

For trans women athletes, at issue is their athletic ability, not their womanhood. If a tournament organizer determines that a trans woman athlete is too good to compete against other women because of her biological advantage, requiring her to compete in an "open" division does not undermine her humanity.

Instead, this acknowledges—and takes seriously—that she identifies as a woman, but that respect for the principles of fair competition requires that she not be allowed to compete in the women's division.

While whatever decision is made is unlikely to make all competitors happy, this approach seems to be the most fair and feasible given the relatively small number of transgender athletes and the unique circumstances of each athlete.

LGBTQIA+ Rights

Periodical and Internet Sources Bibliography

The following articles have been selected to supplement the diverse views presented in this chapter.

Tara Bahrampour, Scott Clement, and Emily Guskin, "Most Americans Oppose Trans Athletes in Female Sports, Poll Finds," *Washington Post*, June 14, 2022. https://www.washingtonpost.com/dc-md-va/2022/06/13/washington-post-umd-poll-most-americans-oppose-transgender-athletes-female-sports.

Rod Dreher, "The Trans-formation of Women's Sports," *American Conservative*, June 6, 2016. https://www.theamericanconservative.com/the-trans-formation-of-womens-sports/.

Tinbete Ermyas and Kira Wakeam, "Wave of Bills to Block Trans Athletes Has No Basis in Science, Researcher Says," NPR, March 18, 2021. https://www.npr.org/2021/03/18/978716732/wave-of-new-bills-say-trans-athletes-have-an-unfair-edge-what-does-the-science-s.

Ugla Stefanía Kristjönudóttir Jónsdóttir, "Roller Derby and Its Wonderful Inclusivity Sets an Example for All Sport," *Metro*, October 9, 2019. https://metro.co.uk/2019/10/09/the-roller-derby-and-its-wonderful-inclusivity-must-be-protected-at-all-costs-10877020/.

Jeré Longman, "Understanding the Controversy over Caster Semenya," *New York Times*, August 18, 2016. https://www.nytimes.com/2016/08/20/sports/caster-semenya-800-meters.html.

Brooke Migdon, "Lia Thomas: 'Trans Women Are Not A Threat to Women's Sports,'" *Hill*, May 31, 2022. https://thehill.com/changing-america/respect/diversity-inclusion/3506803-lia-thomas-trans-women-are-not-a-threat-to-womens-sports/.

Dan Roan and Katie Falkingham, "Transgender Athletes: What Do the Scientists Say?" BBC Sport, May 11, 2022. https://www.bbc.com/sport/61346517.

Nathan J. Robinson, "The Arguments Against Trans Athletes Are Bigoted and Irrational," *Current Affairs*, May 31, 2021. https://www.currentaffairs.org/2021/05/the-arguments-against-trans-athletes-are-bigoted-and-irrational.

Eric Spitznagel, "Trans Women Athletes Have Unfair Advantage over Those Born Female: Testosterone," *New York Post*, July 10, 2021. https://nypost.com/2021/07/10/trans-women-athletes-have-unfair-advantage-over-those-born-female/.

Jack Turban, "Trans Girls Belong on Girls' Sports Teams: There Is No Scientific Case for Excluding Them," *Scientific American*, March 16, 2021. https://www.scientificamerican.com/article/trans-girls-belong-on-girls-sports-teams/.

Tricia Ward, "Do Trans Women Athletes Have Advantages?" WebMD, July 15, 2021. https://www.webmd.com/fitness-exercise/news/20210715/do-trans-women-athletes-have-advantages.

OPPOSING VIEWPOINTS® SERIES

CHAPTER 3

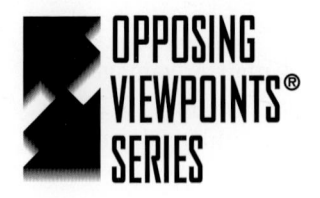

How Do LGBTQIA+ Rights Affect Health Care and Safety?

Chapter Preface

When it comes to rights for LGBTQIA+ people, there are many issues to be debated and resolved. We've seen a few of them already in this volume. And we've seen that LGBTQIA+ people are facing increasing challenges to their rights. Besides being unfair, being denied one's rights can negatively affect one's health and safety. Often it can do more harm than we might realize. Sometimes it can be a matter of life and death. This becomes most obvious when one looks at the high rate of suicide among LGBTQIA+ people, especially LGBTQIA+ youth. But there are other ways anti-LGBTQIA+ policies and attitudes can endanger LGBTQIA+ lives. Health care is one area where LGBTQIA+ people face a great deal of discrimination. Not only do they often find it difficult to get health care or health insurance, but they also find that physicians and other health care workers often lack education about LGBTQIA+ issues, and in far too many cases, they themselves harbor anti-LGBTQIA+ attitudes. A lack of health care or substandard health care can be deadly.

In this chapter, the authors look closely at this issue. They zero in on what LGBTQIA+ discrimination looks like in health care and the effects it has on LGBTQIA+ people. In addition, some of these voices suggest changes that can be made to improve the situation for LGBTQIA+ people, and maybe save lives. One viewpoint also considers the heightened risk of hate crimes in the LGBTQIA+ community.

The news is not all bad, though. Viewpoints here also point out that while there has been a slew of recent state-level anti-LGBTQIA+ legislation, there have been some gains as well, particularly on the federal level. When it comes to health care, the passage of the Affordable Care Act has made it possible for most Americans, including LGBTQIA+ individuals, to have access to health care, and that has saved many lives.

VIEWPOINT 1

> *"Like other populations affected by health disparities, LGBTQ+ people— and transgender and gender diverse (TGD) people in particular—are susceptible to structural (e.g., laws and policies) and interpersonal (e.g., discrimination, harassment) stigma, which undermine their health and wellbeing."*

LGBTQIA+ People Still Face Discrimination in Health Care

Jessica N. Fish

In this viewpoint, Dr. Jennifer N. Fish explains research she has conducted on health disparities in LGBTQIA+ populations— especially LGBTQIA+ youth—and offers suggestions on how to address these issues. According to a large body of research, LGBTQIA+ people face higher levels of mental health and substance abuse issues compared to cisgender and heterosexual people. New research also indicates that these disparities begin at a young age. Discrimination on a structural level as well as in personal relationships plays a major role in causing this inequality, so promoting policies that protect LGBTQIA+ people of all ages and ensure they have access to quality health care can help address it. Dr. Jennifer N. Fish is an assistant professor of family science at the University of Maryland.

"Health Disparities Affecting LGBTQ+ Populations," by Jennifer N. Fish, Communications Medicine, June 9, 2022. https://www.nature.com/articles/s43856-022-00128-1. Licensed under CC BY 4.0 International.

How Do LGBTQIA+ Rights Affect Health Care and Safety?

As you read, consider the following questions:

1. At what age do children start to experience LGBTQIA+-related disparities in mental health, according to research cited in this viewpoint?
2. According to this viewpoint, how does living in a state with fewer laws protecting LGBTQIA+ people affect mental health for LGBTQIA+ youth?
3. What are some recommendations Fish offers for how health care and health policy can be changed to better help LGBTQIA+ people?

Dr. Jessica N. Fish is an Assistant Professor in the Department of Family Science, University of Maryland Prevention Research Center, University of Maryland, USA. Her research seeks to promote the positive development and health of LGBTQ+ people and their families. In this Q&A, Dr. Fish provides insight into the health disparities that affect LGBTQ+ populations, with a particular focus on mental health and the development of LGBTQ+ youth, and important research and policy considerations in this area.

Q: What kind of health issues disproportionately impact LGBTQ+ people at different points in their lives?

A: There is now a compelling body of science that documents elevated risk for a host of poor mental health and substance use outcomes among LGBTQ+ populations compared to their cisgender and heterosexual peers. This includes elevated rates of suicidal ideation and behavior, depression, anxiety, and higher rates of alcohol, tobacco, marijuana, and polysubstance use. Although more research is needed to assess when these disparities emerge across the life course, recent studies find LGBTQ+-related disparities in mental health as young as 10 years old and substance use as young as 12. These findings suggest that youth are aware of feeling different at a very young age and we need to consider how to support and affirm children who later understand themselves to be LGBTQ+. This could include simple alterations to classroom language and activities that acknowledge diverse family structures (e.g., having two moms or dads) and gender expression (e.g., avoid reinforcing specific play activities based on children's assigned sex). Medical and mental health providers can also work with families to normalize children's exploration of gender and gender expression. Acknowledging sexual orientation and gender diversity in a developmentally appropriate way can normalize these experiences and helps to eliminate shame and stigma.

Q: Do we understand the reasons underlying these disparities?

A: Like other populations affected by health disparities, LGBTQ+ people—and transgender and gender diverse (TGD) people in particular—are susceptible to structural (e.g., laws and policies) and interpersonal (e.g., discrimination, harassment) stigma, which undermine their health and wellbeing. This includes barriers to accessing resources like housing and healthcare. For example, LGB youth who live in states with fewer protective policies (e.g., anti-bullying or anti-discrimination policies that name sexual orientation as a protected status) show higher rates of suicidal ideation and behavior. We also know that LGBTQ+ people who experience discrimination and victimization are more likely to report poorer mental health and greater substance use. Unfortunately, these experiences with stigma are typical for LGBTQ+ people and start early in the life course, often from family and peers.

Q: What research is needed to better understand these disparities and how they impact LGBTQ+ people?

A: At this point, LGBTQ+-related health disparities and their link to stigma are well-established. What lags is the implementation of promising strategies to address—and, more importantly, prevent—

these inequities across multiple sectors (e.g., education, healthcare, mental health services). For example, if LGBTQ+-related disparities in mental health are present by age 10, we need to consider how schools can affirm and normalize sexual and gender diversity before middle school and high school. A requisite component to addressing LGBTQ+-related health inequities is to assure that medical and mental health professionals receive adequate training to work with LGBTQ+ clients, including LGBTQ+ youth and their families.

Q: How does your own research further these goals?

A: A main focus of my research seeks to understand how experiences within schools, families, and communities shape the development and health of LGBTQ+ young people and inform strategies (e.g., policies, programs) that promote health. More recently, with the University of Maryland Prevention Research Center (UMD-PRC), I am working with researchers and clinicians to develop and evaluate a comprehensive training program for community mental health organizations and therapists to increase their cultural competence when serving LGBTQ+ clients. Compared to the general population, LGBTQ+ people are more likely to engage with mental healthcare services, but often report experiences with uninformed service providers who perpetuate stereotypes or cause harm in the therapeutic process. We are currently wrapping up a randomized controlled trial and are seeing some promising results regarding the effectiveness of our training program. We hope to be able to offer our training more broadly to help address the lack of required LGBTQ+ training in clinical graduate programs and circumvent the current services gap for LGBTQ+ populations. Generally, we need concerted research, advocacy, and training to address barriers to adequate mental and medical care for LGBTQ+ populations.

Q: What changes do you think are needed, within healthcare or health policy, to begin to address these issues?

A: The current deluge of anti-transgender policies being proposed and enacted across the United States is a horrific example of how policy is being used to harm TGD young people. The science is clear[1,2]: access to gender-affirming care is associated with better mental health for TGD youth (and adults). Policymakers need to ensure that TGD youth have access to developmentally appropriate, gender-affirmative healthcare, including puberty suppression, gender-affirming hormones, and mental health support for TGD youth. Healthcare systems and providers can also advocate for insurance to cover developmentally appropriate, gender-affirmative healthcare. These efforts can be further supported by ensuring that medical providers receive adequate training in working with TGD clients so as not to perpetuate harm when providing services. Ultimately, LGBTQ+ people need policies to protect and ensure their rights to adequate and affirming healthcare. This will require substantive changes in provider training, service administration, and state-level policy. These efforts should be addressed in genuine partnership with LGBTQ+ community members and advocates.

References

1. Toomey R. B., McGuire J. K., Olson K. R., Baams L., & Fish J. N. *Gender-affirming policies support transgender and gender diverse youth's health* (Society for Research in Child Development Statement of the Evidence, 2022); https://www.srcd.org/sites/default/files/resources/SRCD%20SOTE-Gender%20Affirming%20Policies%202022.pdf
2. Rafferty, J., Committee on Psychosocial Aspects of Child and Family Health, Committee on Adolescence. et al. Ensuring comprehensive care and support for transgender and gender-diverse children and adolescents. *Pediatrics* 142, e20182162, (2018).

VIEWPOINT 2

> "Voluntary and community organisations run by and for LGBTQ people fill an important gap. Research shows that social support from volunteers or counsellors who identify as LGBTQ is uniquely beneficial, given their personal connection and insight."

Disparities Exist in Mental Health Care for LGBTQIA+ People

Willem Stander

In this viewpoint, Willem Stander explains how the COVID-19 pandemic disproportionately affected mental health for LGBTQIA+ people and pointed to the need for more specialist support. The COVID-19 pandemic caused many LGBTQIA+ people to feel trapped in unsupportive environments without access to mainstream mental health care. Even online mental health resources have been lacking for LGBTQIA+ people, as most do not cater to the needs of people in these populations. LGBTQIA+ volunteer organizations and charities play an important role in providing mental health support that is lacking in mainstream mental health care. Willem Stander is a research fellow at the University of Birmingham in the United Kingdom.

"LGBTQ People Urgently Need Specialist Mental Health Support—but It Is Lacking," by Willem Stander, The Conversation, June 23, 2020. https://theconversation.com/lgbtq-people-urgently-need-specialist-mental-health-support-but-it-is-lacking-141059. Licensed under CC BY ND 4.0 International.

LGBTQIA+ Rights

As you read, consider the following questions:

1. According to research cited in this viewpoint, where do many gay and bisexual men first go for mental health support?
2. What percent of LGBTQIA+ people surveyed in the study cited in this viewpoint said it was "not at all easy" to find mental health support?
3. What effect did the pandemic have on LGBTQIA+ charities?

The coronavirus pandemic has resulted in a significant rise in demand for mental health support.

LGBTQ people are especially in need of this support, as research suggests that their mental health may be disproportionately affected by the pandemic. Mental health charities offering specialist care for LGBTQ people have already seen an increase in demand for their services. However, this specialist care remains limited.

My PhD research shows the importance of this specialist support. I have found that gay and bisexual men often seek specialist online services as their first source of mental health support—and many participants in my study only sought this help when they were in severe distress or at a crisis. This demonstrates the urgent need for relevant and appropriate support aimed at LGBTQ people.

Increase in Demand

A report by the LGBT Foundation has pinpointed issues that may put LGBTQ people at risk of being severely affected by the coronavirus crisis. LGBT people are more likely to face mental health difficulties, homelessness and domestic abuse when compared to the general population.

In addition, many LGBTQ people may be caught in unsupportive or abusive environments as a result of safety measures such as social distancing and self-isolation. They may either have to come out to potentially unsupportive family or hide part of their identity.

However, LBGTQ people face barriers in accessing mainstream mental healthcare. A recent national LGBT survey by the UK government revealed that 28% of respondents found it "not at all easy" to access mental health support. When they did get mental health support, 22% reported a negative experience.

Worryingly, some respondents had been offered harmful treatments such as conversion therapy, most often by faith groups but also by healthcare professionals—despite condemnation of this treatment by major counselling and psychotherapy bodies and the NHS. A 2015 Stonewall report also suggested that some health and social care workers lack confidence in their ability to understand and respond to the needs of LGBTQ people.

These challenges also extend to online support. For example, a review of web and mobile phone resources for depression and anxiety suggests that they are largely aimed at heterosexual users and seldom cater to the needs of LGBTQ people. These resources fail to address issues that are common to this community, such as coming out and coping with experiences of discrimination or harassment. Few include referrals to mental health services that specifically focus on the LGBTQ community.

Limited Funding

Voluntary and community organisations run by and for LGBTQ people fill an important gap. Research shows that social support from volunteers or counsellors who identify as LGBTQ is uniquely beneficial, given their personal connection and insight.

During the coronavirus pandemic, charities focused on the mental health of the LGBTQ community, such as MindOut, have continued to provide essential services online. These include emotional support, information and direction to further resources.

However, the pandemic has seen these charities report a sharp fall in community fundraising events and other forms of planned income, as well as a loss of volunteers.

This is evident in the results of a survey carried out by Consortium, a specialist infrastructure charity supporting

LGBTQ groups and organisations. According to the survey findings, many of their members are reporting a loss or reduction in grant funding, donations and other sources of income. This has resulted in a reduction of staff hours and services among some organisations.

The UK government has allocated a £750 million support package to help charities across the UK continue their vital work during the pandemic. However, Consortium's survey reveals that a majority of its members have been unable to access any of the government support schemes and some are fearing imminent closure.

The cancellation of Pride events is also a major setback for fundraising efforts and those organisations who benefit from corporate partnerships such as proceeds from special merchandise or products. As a result, several charities such as the Allsorts Youth Project and London Friend have launched crowdfunding initiatives to help maintain and expand their online services.

In light of increased demand and the ongoing need for specialist services, it is vital that LGBTQ charities continue offering support to those in need for the duration of the coronavirus pandemic and beyond. It is likely that these charities will need to rely on donations to ensure that those who are the most vulnerable and marginalised among us are able to access relevant and appropriate support.

VIEWPOINT 3

> "Many transgender people are hesitant to engage with clinicians and medical office staff due to a personal history of mistreatment by the medical community."

The Ethics of Who Should Provide Gender-Affirming Care Are Complex

Cary S. Crall and Rachel K. Jackson

One of today's most hotly debated topics about LGBTQIA+ rights is whether or not psychiatrists and medical doctors should provide gender-affirming treatments to transgender adolescents—though research suggests it is often a matter of life and death for trans kids and teens. In this excerpted viewpoint, the authors analyze a case-study of a psychiatrist trying to decide if he should handle his patient's treatment himself. At the time this viewpoint was published, Rachel K. Jackson was a fourth-year medical student at the University of Washington in Seattle and Cary S. Crall, MD, was a first-year resident physician at the Massachusetts General Hospital.

"Should Psychiatrists Prescribe Gender-Affirming Hormone Therapy to Transgender Adolescents?" by Cary S. Crall and Rachel K. Jackson, AMA Journal of Ethics, November 2016. Excerpt reprinted by permission and the full article is available at: https://journalofethics.ama-assn.org/article/should-psychiatrists-prescribe-gender-affirming-hormone-therapy-transgender-adolescents/2016-11.

As you read, consider the following questions:

1. What particular concerns did Jessie have about her transition, as described here? Why did she want Dr. Lao to administer the therapy himself?
2. What challenges do doctors face when deciding about treatment for patients like Jessie?
3. What are the authors' conclusions about the dilemma Dr. Lao faces?

In the medium-sized city where he practices psychiatry, Dr. Lao has developed expertise in treating and counseling transgender adolescents. This afternoon, Dr. Lao is scheduled to meet with Jessie, a 15-year-old high school student with autism spectrum disorder. Jessie has been Dr. Lao's patient since elementary school. Within the last two years, Jessie, who was birth-assigned male, began opening up to her family and Dr. Lao about her identity as a transgender female.

In the waiting room, Jessie's parents pulled Dr. Lao aside. "Is it true that you will soon start administering hormone therapy yourself?" Jessie's father asked Dr. Lao. "Because it would be great if we didn't have to find another physician when Jessie starts hormone treatment. Jessie said she would much rather have you perform the treatments."

It was true that Dr. Lao was considering becoming trained to administer hormone therapy. Many of Dr. Lao's transgender patients and families have complained about the lack of physicians in their rural community who are trained in hormone therapy administration. Dr. Lao thought he might play a role in reducing this resource disparity for his patients by becoming trained himself.

Their previous session ended just as Jessie began to describe some of her anxieties to Dr. Lao about transitioning from male to female. Jessie worried about what her classmates might think about her transition, and, while her immediate family was very supportive, Jessie worried about the opinions of members of her extended family, who tended to be less progressive on issues of gender and sexuality.

In their session today, Dr. Lao wanted to follow up with Jessie about these concerns. "Jessie, when we last met, you mentioned concerns regarding how your classmates and family members might react to your transition—would you like to keep discussing that?" With that question, Dr. Lao noticed that Jessie seemed somewhat withdrawn and uncharacteristically uncomfortable in front of him. "No," she replied, "I thought it over, and I'm not as worried anymore about what they'll think." Dr. Lao tried a couple more times in their discussion—with little success—to veer the conversation back to Jessie's formerly expressed worries about her transition. At the end of their session, Jessie said to Dr. Lao before leaving his office, "I'm feeling very ready to begin hormones—and it would make me so happy if you were the one managing my treatments, Dr. Lao."

As Dr. Lao waved goodbye to Jessie and her family, he couldn't help but wonder if Jessie's refusal to discuss her anxieties about her transition were related to her wish to pursue hormone therapy under his care. Could it be that Jessie feared Dr. Lao would be hesitant to treat her or might delay the process if Jessie disclosed her anxieties about transitioning with him? Dr. Lao wondered: If he developed expertise in hormone therapy, would his patients then perceive him as a kind of gatekeeper in the process of their transition? Will his role in offering hormone therapy sacrifice important elements in his therapeutic relationships with his patients like Jessie?

Commentary

Initiating and managing care for transgender patients can often be daunting, even for a caring, motivated physician like Dr. Lao. Transgender people who seek gender-affirming medical care are a small, geographically diffuse community with specialized medical needs requiring coordinated communication among multiple medical specialists. They experience rampant social discrimination, often leading to unemployment and unequal access to health insurance [1] as well as high rates of mental illness [2], further complicating their ability to obtain adequate care. Additionally, many transgender people are hesitant to engage with clinicians and medical office staff due to a personal history of mistreatment by the medical community. [...]

These challenges have led to a system in which transgender care is centralized in specialized, cross-disciplinary health clinics located in major cities, leaving the most vulnerable transgender patients—those from racial or ethnic minority communities, of low socioeconomic status, or young or elderly people living in rural communities—largely without quality care. What is the nature and scope of an individual psychiatrist's obligation to provide gender-affirming medical treatment to patients seeking hormone therapy, especially when providing such care can extend beyond his or her normal scope of practice?

As is the case with many medical interventions, Dr. Lao's decision to provide hormone therapy is clinically and ethically complex. Careful analysis guided by the principles of patient autonomy, beneficence, nonmaleficence, and justice provides an overall framework to guide psychiatrists, particularly those in rural communities, on how they should proceed.

Ethical Principles Favoring Hormone Therapy Administration

The principles of patient autonomy and beneficence support the need for psychiatrists to prescribe hormone therapy for gender-transitioning adolescents.

Patient autonomy. The patient autonomy argument for providing HRT is straightforward—physicians should honor transgender patients' right to express their gender identity by providing desired medical interventions in line with the established standard of care [3, 4]. [...]

Beneficence. The principle of beneficence—the obligation to do good for the patient—additionally supports Dr. Lao's providing hormone therapy. The best available evidence, along with decades of clinical experience, indicates that effective hormone therapy has a positive effect on psychological and quality of life outcomes in transgender people [5]. Jessie's anxiety and depression plants her firmly within the mainstream for young transgender people who live with varying degrees of social, legal, and medical affirmation of their gender identity.

[…]

The causal pathway to higher rates of mental illness in transgender youth is illuminated by a recent study, which found that socially transitioned transgender children who are supported in their gender identity have developmentally normal levels of depression and only minimal elevations in anxiety compared to other children their age [6]. This finding suggests that psychopathology within this group is a product of poor social acceptance rather than an intrinsic part of transgender identity. Pubertal suppression and hormone therapy are the chief tools physicians have at their disposal for minimizing a transgender patient's risk of suffering adverse mental health outcomes.

Opportunities to provide benefit to the patient extend well beyond psychological care as Jessie, at age 16, is undergoing physical development that requires timely medical intervention to maximize medical affirmation of her gender identity. […] In the absence of other physicians willing to provide hormone treatment, Dr. Lao's obligation to intervene based on the principle of beneficence is imperative to Jessie's well-being.

Ethical Principles that Do Not Support Psychiatric Administration of Hormone Therapy

Ethical analysis based on the principles of nonmaleficence and justice suggests that Dr. Lao should think twice before providing hormone therapy for gender-transitioning adolescents.

Nonmaleficence. Although there are strong arguments in favor of Dr. Lao being trained to provide gender-affirming medical care, specifically hormone therapy, the ethical principles of nonmaleficence and justice weigh on the other side of the balance. Nonmaleficence—to do no harm—is a complicated standard to uphold in this case. [...]

Dr. Lao must be prepared to monitor and treat all side effects of the medications he prescribes, whether through his own efforts or expert consultation. Unfortunately, he is unlikely to have been taught basic hormone therapy administration or pubertal suppression while completing his psychiatry residency training. [...] Because Dr. Lao is practicing in a rural setting without access to transgender-affirming medical specialists for consultation, he must consider the potential harm to Jessie of initiating hormone therapy and then being required to stop if complications arise that he does not have the expertise to manage.

Additionally, because Dr. Lao is Jessie's psychiatrist, he must consider the potential harm to his therapeutic alliance with her if he chooses to prescribe hormone therapy. On the one hand, the standard of care for prescribing hormone therapy, especially in adolescents, calls for invasive physical exams, including of breast and genital tissue—a practice that could generate negative transference reactions from Dr. Lao or Jessie and be detrimental to the therapeutic relationship. On the other hand, as Jessie's mental health clinician, Dr. Lao has an obligation to help Jessie process her gender dysphoria, regardless of whether she chooses to continue medical assistance with her transition. If Dr. Lao is invested in managing Jessie's hormone therapy, will he be able to integrate the physical dimensions of her care into their therapeutic relationship without causing harm?

Justice. Finally, the principle of distributive justice—the fair distribution of scarce resources and the balancing of competing needs—calls into question the ethical and clinical wisdom of Dr. Lao taking on the responsibility of prescribing hormone therapy. While providing hormone therapy would serve to bring this resource to a population in which there is a relative scarcity of access, Dr. Lao's position as a psychiatrist who sees adolescents in a rural area makes his time another scarce resource to consider. [...] Long wait times for patients with high-acuity chief complaints, ranging from first-episode psychosis to posttraumatic stress disorder (PTSD) from chronic abuse, would potentially increase if a clinician unfamiliar with a relatively rare condition took time to learn its management. Is there truly a clinical and ethical imperative for Dr. Lao to take on learning to serve outside his current scope of practice when the need for him to serve within its limits is already so great?

[…]

References

1. Movement Advancement Project; Human Rights Campaign; Center for American Progress. *A Broken Bargain: Discrimination, Fewer Benefits and More Taxes for LGBT Workers.* http://www.lgbtmap.org/file/a-broken-bargain-full-report.pdf. Published June 2013. Accessed September 7, 2016.
2. Reisner SL, Biello KB, White Hughto JM, et al. Psychiatric diagnoses and comorbidities in a diverse, multicity cohort of young transgender women: baseline findings from Project LifeSkills. *JAMA Pediatr* 2016;170(5):481-486.
3. Coleman E, Bockting W, Botzer M, et al. Standards of care for the health of transsexual, transgender, and gender-nonconforming people, version 7. *Int J Transgend* 2012;13(4):165-232.
4. Hembree WC, Cohen-Kettenis P, Delemarre-van de Waal HA, et al; Endocrine Society. Endocrine treatment of transsexual persons: an Endocrine Society clinical practice guideline. *J Clin Endocrinol Metab.* 2009;94(9):3132-3154.
5. White Hughto JM, Reisner SL. A systematic review of the effects of hormone therapy on psychological functioning and quality of life in transgender individuals. *Transgend Health* 2016;1(1):21-31.
6. Olson KR, Durwood L, DeMeules M, McLaughlin KA. Mental health of transgender children who are supported in their identities. *Pediatrics.* 2016;137(3):e20153223. http://pediatrics.aappublications.org/content/137/3/e20153223.long.Accessed September 28, 2016.

VIEWPOINT 4

> "The Trevor Project estimates that more than 1.8 million LGBTQ youth (13-24) seriously consider suicide each year in the U.S. — and at least one attempts suicide every 45 seconds."

LGBTQIA+ Youth Face Higher Risk of Suicide
The Trevor Project

This viewpoint from the Trevor Project considers statistics about the risk of suicide among LGBTQIA+ youth that were collected by the organization as well as in other studies. The data clearly indicates that LGBTQIA+ youth experience higher rates of suicide attempts than heterosexual youth. LGBTQIA+ youth of color experience even higher rates, pointing to the role of intersectionality in unequal mental health care. The viewpoint also examines the role of some risk factors for LGBTQIA+ youth suicide, including bullying, discrimination, and rejection or lack of support. The Trevor Project is an American nonprofit organization focused on suicide prevention for LGBTQIA+ youth.

As you read, consider the following questions:

1. What percent of LGBTQIA+ youth considered attempting suicide, as reported in the Trevor Project's 2022 National Survey on LGBTQ Youth Mental?

"Facts About LGBTQ Youth Suicide," The Trevor Project, December 15, 2021. Reprinted by permission.

2. How is intersectionality defined in this viewpoint?
3. According to this viewpoint, what does the Minority Stress Model suggest?

LGBTQ youth are not inherently prone to suicide risk because of their sexual orientation or gender identity but rather placed at higher risk because of how they are mistreated and stigmatized in society.

Top-Line Statistics

- Suicide is the second leading cause of death among young people aged 10 to 24 (Hedegaard, Curtin, & Warner, 2018) — and lesbian, gay, bisexual, transgender, queer, and questioning (LGBTQ) youth are at significantly increased risk.
- LGBTQ youth are more than four times as likely to attempt suicide than their peers (Johns et al., 2019; Johns et al., 2020).
- The Trevor Project estimates that more than 1.8 million LGBTQ youth (13-24) seriously consider suicide each year in the U.S.—and at least one attempts suicide every 45 seconds.
- The Trevor Project's 2022 National Survey on LGBTQ Youth Mental Health found that 45% of LGBTQ youth seriously considered attempting suicide in the past year, including more than half of transgender and nonbinary youth.

The Importance of Intersectionality

- Intersectionality is a framework for understanding how interdependent and multidimensional social identities at the individual level, such as race/ethnicity, gender, and sexuality, are shaped by interlocking systems of privilege and oppression at the societal level, such as heterosexism, cisgenderism, and racism (Crenshaw, 1991).
- This intersection of identities may, in turn, present distinct stressors for some LGBTQ youth compared to others, and

LGBTQIA+ Rights

minority stress may be most persistent and problematic for youth who occupy multiple marginalized social positions (Cyrus, 2017).
- That said, largely due to sample size limitations, researchers often fail to examine within-group differences among LGBTQ youth, limiting our understanding of within-group disparities in suicidal thoughts and behaviors.
- However, existing research points to increased disparities for bisexual youth, transgender and nonbinary youth, and LGBTQ youth of color.

Mental Health Disparities Across Social Identities

Bisexual Youth

- Data shows that bisexual youth, or those who have the capacity to form attraction and/or relationships to more than one gender, report higher rates of depressed mood, bullying, sexual assault, and physical harm.
- According to The Trevor Project's analysis of CDC data, almost half (48%) of bi young people seriously considered attempting suicide in the past year, and 27% attempted suicide. Among gay or lesbian youth, 37% seriously considered suicide and 19% attempted. And among straight youth, 14% seriously considered suicide and 6% attempted suicide.
- These suicide risk disparities among bi youth also remain constant across gender identity and race/ethnicity.

Transgender and Nonbinary Youth

- Transgender and nonbinary youth face elevated risk for depression, thoughts of suicide, and attempting suicide compared to youth who are cisgender and straight, including cisgender members of the LGBTQ community.
- A 2020 peer-reviewed study by The Trevor Project's researchers, published in the *Journal of Adolescent Health*,

found that transgender and nonbinary youth were 2 to 2.5 times as likely to experience depressive symptoms, seriously consider suicide, and attempt suicide compared to their cisgender LGBQ peers.

LGBTQ Youth of Color

- The Trevor Project's 2022 national survey found that LGBTQ youth of color reported higher rates of attempting suicide than their white peers in the past year. Among the nearly 34,000 LGBTQ youth surveyed, 12% of white youth attempted suicide compared to 21% of Native/Indigenous youth, 20% of Middle Eastern/Northern African youth, 19% of Black youth, 17% of multiracial youth, 16% of Latinx youth, and 12% of Asian/Pacific Islander youth.
- Across race/ethnicity, Native/Indigenous youth who are Two-Spirit/LGBTQ consistently report the highest suicide risk.
- The Trevor Project's research has found that they were 2.5 times more likely to report a suicide attempt in the past year (33%) compared to their LGBTQ peers (14%). Additionally, this group is also disproportionately represented in reports of foster care, housing instability, and food insecurity.
- In particular, Black transgender and nonbinary youth report disproportionate rates of suicide risk — with 59% seriously considering suicide and more than 1 in 4 (26%) attempting suicide in the past year.
- These disparities highlight the devastating impacts of historical and ongoing oppression and trauma inflicted on Black, Indigenous, and people of color.

Some Key Risk Factors for LGBTQ Youth Suicide

Minority Stress

- The Minority Stress Model, one of the most predominant theories used to explain mental health disparities experienced by LGBTQ individuals, suggests that experiences of LGBTQ-based victimization—and the internalization of these experiences and anti-LGBTQ messages—can compound and produce negative mental health outcomes and increase suicide risk among LGBTQ individuals (Meyer, 2003).
- A 2021 peer-reviewed study by The Trevor Project's researchers, published in the *American Journal of Community Psychology*, found that greater experiences of minority stress experiences are associated with increased odds of attempting suicide. LGBTQ youth who reported experiencing four types of minority stress—LGBTQ-based physical harm, discrimination, housing instability, and change attempts by parents—were 12 times at greater odds of attempting suicide compared to youth who experienced none.

Rejection and Lack of Social Support and Affirming Spaces

- Research suggests that among LGBTQ youth, only one-third experience parental acceptance, with an additional one-third experiencing parental rejection, and the final one-third not disclosing their LGBTQ identity until they are adults (Katz-Wise et al., 2015). Another study found that LGB young adults who report high levels of parental rejection are eight times more likely to report attempting suicide and six times more likely to report high levels of depression (Ryan et al., 2009).
- Many LGBTQ youth lack access to affirming spaces, with only 55% of LGBTQ youth reporting that their school is LGBTQ-affirming and only 37% saying that their home

is LGBTQ-affirming. Fewer than 1 in 3 transgender and nonbinary youth found their home to be gender-affirming and a little more than half (51%) found their school to be affirming. The Trevor Project's research consistently finds that LGBTQ young people report lower rates of attempting suicide when they have access to LGBTQ-affirming spaces.

Physical Harm and Bullying

- 36% of LGBTQ youth reported that they have been physically threatened or harmed, and those who did attempted suicide at nearly triple the rate of those who did not in the past year.
- The Trevor Project's research has also found that 52% of LGBTQ youth who were enrolled in middle or high school reported being bullied either in person or electronically in the past year, and those who did had three times greater odds of attempting suicide in the past year.

Discrimination

- 73% of LGBTQ youth report that they had experienced discrimination based on their sexual orientation or gender identity at least once in their lifetime, and those who did attempted suicide at more than twice the rate of those who did not in the past year.
- A 2020 peer-reviewed study by The Trevor Project's researchers, published in the *Journal of Adolescent Health*, found that transgender and nonbinary youth who report experiencing discrimination based on their gender identity had more than double the odds of attempting suicide in the past year compared to those who did not experience discrimination based on their gender identity.

Conversion Therapy

- A 2020 peer-reviewed study by The Trevor Project's researchers, published in the *American Journal of Public Health*, found that youth who reported undergoing conversion therapy were more than twice as likely to report having attempted suicide and more than 2.5 times as likely to report multiple suicide attempts in the past year.
- According to The Trevor Project's 2022 national survey of nearly 34,000 diverse LGBTQ youth ages 13-24 across the U.S., 17% reported being threatened with or subjected to conversion therapy, including more than 1 in 5 transgender and nonbinary youth and more than 1 in 10 cisgender youth.

Some Key Protective Factors for LGBTQ Youth Suicide

Social Support and Acceptance from Adults and Peers

- Having at least one accepting adult can reduce the risk of a suicide attempt among LGBTQ young people by 40 percent.
- A 2021 peer-reviewed study by The Trevor Project's researchers, published in *Transgender Health*, found that transgender and nonbinary youth who reported gender identity acceptance from adults and peers had significantly lower odds of attempting suicide in the past year.
- LGBTQ youth who felt high social support from their family reported attempting suicide at less than half the rate of those who felt low or moderate social support.
- LGBTQ youth who live in a community that is accepting of LGBTQ people reported much lower rates of attempting suicide than those who do not.

Affirming Spaces and Activities, Especially at School

- The Trevor Project's research has found that LGBTQ youth who found their school and home to be LGBTQ-affirming reported lower rates of attempting suicide.
- LGBTQ youth who report the presence of trusted adults in their school have higher levels of self-esteem (Dessel et al., 2017) and access to supportive peers is protective against anxiety and depression, including among those who lack support from their family (Parra et al., 2018).
- Schools also offer youth the ability to participate in extracurricular activities and clubs, which have been found to promote positive youth development (Eccles et al., 2003). The presence of Gender and Sexualities Alliances (GSAs) has been found to significantly reduce the risk for depression and increase well-being among LGBTQ youth and young adults (Toomey et al., 2011).

Policies and Practices that Support Transgender and Nonbinary Youth

- Transgender and nonbinary youth attempt suicide less when their pronouns are respected, when they are allowed to officially change the gender marker on their legal documents, and when they have access to spaces (online, at school, and home) that affirm their gender identity.
- Transgender and nonbinary youth who reported having pronouns respected by all or most people in their lives attempted suicide at half the rate of those who did not have their pronouns respected.
- A 2022 peer-reviewed study by The Trevor Project researchers, published in the *International Journal of Environmental Research and Public Health*, found that transgender and nonbinary youth who had changed their legal documents reported significantly lower rates of attempting suicide in the past year compared to those who had not.

- Gender-affirming medical care, such as hormone therapy, is associated with positive mental health outcomes including showing promise for reducing suicide risk. A 2021 peer-reviewed study by The Trevor Project's researchers, published in the *Journal of Adolescent Health*, found that gender-affirming hormone therapy is significantly related to lower rates of depression, suicidal thoughts, and suicide attempts among transgender and nonbinary youth.

References

Crenshaw, K. (1991). Mapping the margins: Intersectionality, identity politics, and violence against women of color. Stanford Law Review, *43*(6), 1241–1299.

Cyrus, K. (2017). Multiple minorities as multiply marginalized: Applying the minority stress theory to LGBTQ people of color. *Journal of Gay & Lesbian Mental Health, 21*(3), 194–202.

DeChants, J. P., Price, M. N., Green, A. E., Davis, C. K., & Pick, C. J. (2022). Association of updating identification documents with suicidal Ideation and attempts among transgender and nonbinary youth. *International Journal of Environmental Research and Public Health, 19*(9), 5016.

Dessel, A. B., Kulick, A., Wernick, L. J., & Sullivan, D. (2017). The importance of teacher support: Differential impacts by gender and sexuality. *Journal of Adolescence, 56*, 136-144.

Eccles, J. S., Barber, B. L., Stone, M., & Hunt, J. (2003). Extracurricular activities and adolescent development. *Journal of Social Issues, 59*(4), 865-889.

Green, A. E., DeChants, J. P., Price, M. N., & Davis, C. K. (2021). Association of gender-affirming hormone therapy with depression, thoughts of suicide, and attempted suicide among transgender and nonbinary youth. *Journal of Adolescent Health*, 1–7.

Green, A. E., Price, M. N., & Dorison, S. H. (2021). Cumulative minority stress and suicide risk among LGBTQ youth. *American Journal of Community Psychology*, 1–12.

Green, A. E., Price-Feeney, M., & Dorison, S.H. (2019). *National Estimate of LGBTQ Youth Seriously Considering Suicide*. New York, New York: The Trevor Project.

Green, A. E., Price-Feeney, M., & Dorison, S. H. (2021). Association of sexual orientation acceptance with reduced suicide attempts among lesbian, gay, bisexual, transgender, queer, and questioning youth. *LGBT health, 8*(1), 26–31.

Green, A. E., Price-Feeney, M., Dorison, S. H., & Pick, C. J. (2020). Self-reported conversion efforts and suicidality among US LGBTQ youths and young adults, 2018. *American Journal of Public Health, 110*(8), 1221–1227.

Hedegaard, H., Curtin, S.C., & Warner, M. (2018). Suicide mortality in the United States, 1999–2017. *National Center for Health Statistics Data Brief, 330*, Hyattsville, MD: National Center for Health Statistics.

Johns, M. M., Lowry, R., Andrzejewski, J., Barrios, L. C., Zewditu, D., McManus, T., et al. (2019). Transgender identity and experiences of violence victimization, substance use, suicide risk, and sexual risk behaviors among high school student–19 states and large urban school districts, 2017. *Morbidity and Mortality Weekly Report, 68*(3), 65-71.

Johns, M. M., Lowry, R., Haderxhanaj, L. T., et al. (2020). Trends in violence victimization and suicide risk by sexual identity among high school students — Youth Risk Behavior Survey, United States, 2015-2019. *Morbidity and Mortality Weekly Report, 69,*(Suppl-1):19–27.

Katz-Wise, S. L., Rosario, M., & Tsappis, M. (2016). Lesbian, gay, bisexual, and transgender youth and family acceptance. *Pediatric Clinics of North America, 63*(6), 1011-1025.

Meyer, I. H. (2003) Prejudice, social stress, and mental health in lesbian, gay, bisexual populations: Conceptual issues and research evidence. *Psychological Bulletin, 129*(5), 674-697.

Parra, L. A., Bell, T. S., Benibgui, M., Helm, J. L., & Hastings, P. D. (2018). The buffering effect of peer support on the links between family rejection and psychosocial adjustment in LGB emerging adults. *Journal of Social and Personal Relationships, 35*(6), 854-871.

Price-Feeney, M., Green, A. E., & Dorison, S. (2020). Understanding the mental health of transgender and nonbinary youth. *Journal of Adolescent Health, 66*(6), 684–690.

Price-Feeney, M., Green, A. E., & Dorison, S. (2020). *All Black Lives Matter: Mental Health of Black LGBTQ Youth.* New York, New York: The Trevor Project.

Price-Feeney, M., Green, A. E., & Dorison, S. H. (2021). Impact of bathroom discrimination on mental health among transgender and nonbinary youth. *Journal of Adolescent Health, 68*(6), 1142–1147.

Ryan, C., Huebner, D., Diaz, R. M., & Sanchez, J. (2009). Family rejection as a predictor of negative health outcomes in white and Latino lesbian, gay, and bisexual young adults. *Pediatrics, 123*(1), 346-352.

The Trevor Project. (2019). *Research Brief: Bisexual Youth Experience.* https://www.thetrevorproject.org/research-briefs/bisexual-youth-experience/

The Trevor Project. (2019). *Research Brief: Accepting Adults Reduce Suicide Attempts Among LGBTQ Youth.* https://www.thetrevorproject.org/research-briefs/accepting-adults-reduce-suicide-attempts-among-lgbtq-youth/

The Trevor Project. (2020). *2020 National Survey on LGBTQ Youth Mental Health.* https://www.thetrevorproject.org/wp-content/uploads/2020/07/The-Trevor-Project-National-Survey-Results-2020.pdf

The Trevor Project. (2020). *Research Brief: American Indian/Alaskan Native Youth Suicide Risk.* https://www.thetrevorproject.org/research-briefs/american-indian-alaskan-native-youth-suicide-risk/

The Trevor Project. (2020). *Research Brief: LGBTQ & Gender-Affirming Spaces.* https://www.thetrevorproject.org/research-briefs/lgbtq-gender-affirming-spaces/

The Trevor Project. (2021). *Research Brief: Bullying and Suicide Risk among LGBTQ Youth.* https://www.thetrevorproject.org/research-briefs/bullying-and-suicide-risk-among-lgbtq-youth/

The Trevor Project. (2021). *Estimate of How Often LGBTQ Youth Attempt Suicide in the U.S.* https://www.thetrevorproject.org/research-briefs/estimate-of-how-often-lgbtq-youth-attempt-suicide-in-the-u-s/

LGBTQIA+ Rights

The Trevor Project. (2021). *2021 National Survey on LGBTQ Youth Mental Health.* https://www.thetrevorproject.org/survey-2022/assets/static/trevor01_2022survey_final.pdf

The Trevor Project. (2022). *2022 National Survey on LGBTQ Youth Mental Health.* https://www.thetrevorproject.org/survey-2022/assets/static/trevor01_2022survey_final.pdf

Toomey, R. B., Ryan, C., Diaz, R. M., & Russell, S. T. (2011). High school gay–straight alliances (GSAs) and young adult well-being: An examination of GSA presence, participation, and perceived effectiveness. *Applied Developmental Science, 15*(4), 175-185.

VIEWPOINT 5

> "Heteronormativity — the assumption that all people are straight — and cis-normativity — the assumption that all people are distinctly either a man or a woman — create many health disparities for 2SLGBTQ+ people. They also create barriers to accessing safe and inclusive care."

Compassionate Care Is Needed to Address Health Inequality in LGBTQIA+ Communities

Phillip Joy, Andrew Thomas, and Megan Aston

In this viewpoint, the authors look at the role of compassion in health care in Canada for 2SLGBTQ+ people, which is the acronym commonly preferred in Canada and stands for Two-Spirit, lesbian, gay, bisexual, transgender, queer, and other sexual identities. Two-Spirit is a term used by some Indigenous North Americans to describe people who have both a masculine and feminine spirit and occupy a distinct alternative gender status. The authors argue that it is difficult for people in 2SLGBTQ+ communities to find compassionate health care and are often exposed to ignorance or prejudice. Through training, these issues can be addressed, and health care professionals can provide more compassionate care. Phillip Joy is an assistant professor of applied human nutrition at Mount Saint Vincent

"Compassion in Health Care Reduces Health Inequality for 2SLBGTQ+ People," by Phillip Joy, Andrew Thomas, and Megan Aston, The Conversation, June 23, 2022. https://theconversation.com/compassion-in-health-care-reduces-health-inequality-for-2slgbtq-people-185191. Licensed under CC BY-ND 4.0 International.

University. Andrew Thomas is a peer-to-peer program coordinator for a harm reduction at the AIDS Coalition of Nova Scotia. Megan Aston is a professor in the school of nursing at Dalhousie University.

As you read, consider the following questions:

1. How is compassion defined in this viewpoint?
2. In terms of time, how much compassionate care from health professionals is enough to have positive benefits on patients?
3. According to this viewpoint, what was the authors' aim in publishing their study in *Qualitative Health Research*?

Compassion is more than being nice and can be viewed in many different ways. Philosophers, religious leaders and scientists from different parts of the world have all discussed the meanings of compassion within their own contexts. It can be described as a distinct emotion, a virtue or a way of life that recognizes the pain and suffering of others. Compassion can be a means to self-healing and feeling our common humanity.

But compassion is also action: a "form of engagement with the world." Compassion has the potential to positively transform social systems or the potential to reinforce current beliefs that can separate people.

Some have even critiqued the concept of compassion, particularly from a Western perspective, as an emotion that is focused on oneself and leads to the comparisons of the self with others.

Within Western health-care systems, there is growing recognition that compassion is an essential component for positive health and well-being. There have been calls for compassion to be a greater part of the care processes of health professions and the training of health professionals.

Researchers have shown that as little as 40 seconds of compassion have made positive differences in patients' experiences and health. In those 40 seconds, compassion can be expressed by acknowledging patient concerns, showing support, acting as a partner and validating emotions.

Compassion and Health Care for 2SLBGTQ+ People

Accessing and receiving compassionate health care, however, is often not possible for many groups, including Two-Spirit, lesbian, gay, bisexual, transgender, queer and other sexual identities, such as pansexual or asexual (2SLGBTQ+) individuals.

Heteronormativity—the assumption that all people are straight—and cis-normativity—the assumption that all people are distinctly either a man or a woman—create many health disparities for 2SLGBTQ+ people. They also create barriers to accessing safe and inclusive care.

Heteronormativity and cis-normativity can lead to fear, ignorance, prejudice and acts of violence towards 2SLGBTQ+ in Canada. Research has shown that education on these topics during training for health-care professionals is beneficial, but physicians have reported a lack of advanced knowledge on 2SLGBTQ+ issues. There is a growing recognition for the need of more 2SLGBTQ+ health training and more funding for 2SLGBTQ+ health research.

Transformative Compassion Study

The aim of our forthcoming research, to be published in the journal *Qualitative Health Research*, was to explore the meanings of compassion for 2SLGBTQ+ individuals.

In our study—carried out at Mount Saint Vincent University—we talked with 20 self-identifying 2SLGBTQ+ people from across Canada. In online interviews, we asked them to share experiences of compassion (or non-compassion) and to tell us about their beliefs and values about compassion. Many of the things our participants shared were about compassion and health.

In our findings, we explored the meanings and expectations of compassion in health care for our participants. As one them said: "Good health care has to have compassion at the core." Several of our participants noted that comfort, safety, inclusive language and awareness and understanding of the shared trauma that many 2SLGBTQ+ individuals suffer are essential components for health care to be compassionate.

Compassionate Health Care Is Not Guaranteed

Another participant believed that when "*…you're accessing the health-care system you would expect compassion from the health-care system. I know a lot of people, queer or not, don't have that experience. Compassion isn't guaranteed in health care, but when it's found it's celebrated.*"

For example, this participant described their experiences during the COVID-19 pandemic in which their doctor showed compassion to them by including their partner:

> "COVID brought out this huge experience of shared humanity among all kinds of different people… a lot of compassion showed through in those first early months, where we're all in this together."

Compassionate Comics

We wanted to share the beliefs and experiences expressed in the study as a means to start conversations about compassion, and to work towards creating awareness about the power of compassion to positively transform the lives, health and well-being. We have previously used comics as a means to share our research, and chose to do so again.

To create our compassionate comics, we enlisted the talents of 12 2SLGBTQ+ artists from Canada, the United States, the United Kingdom and Greece. We asked each of them to illustrate stories told by our participants.

For example, a few participants used the HIV/AIDS crisis as an historic example of both the non-compassion in the health-care system and the power of compassion to change systems.

As one participant related:

"When I was in my 20s, the AIDS crisis was at its peak, and although in the long run I think that inspired compassion among the general public, at the time there was a lot of negativity. A lot of blaming of people, blaming of behaviours. A lot of religious nastiness. So, over time that has changed and I think media had a lot to do with it. And the organization of the queer community during the AIDS crisis—and I think more visibility—humanized people to the general public in a way that hadn't happened before."

This story is reflected in a comic entitled *"Remember"* by Canadian artist David Winters. In the 10-page story, a nurse walks through a crowd of anti-gay protesters outside her hospital to go to work. She shows compassion to a dying man by listening and showing understanding to him when others did not.

Our study results are reflective of only a few voices from the 2SLGBTQ+ umbrella, so we cannot make overarching generalizations. However, we can suggest that compassion was seen as a central and critical component for good care.

We suggest that in order to truly transform health care, we must examine and challenge assumptions of sexuality and gender in health-care practices and systems. Doing this will help all people feel comfort, safety and understanding—in other words, compassion.

VIEWPOINT 6

> "Hate crimes do not just affect an individual — whole communities can be affected by hate. In what's known as 'collective trauma,' LGBTQ people often internalize the violence inflicted on other members of the community."

LGBTQIA+ People Face a Heightened Risk of Hate Crimes

Andrew Ryan Flores, Ilan Meyer, and Rebecca Stotzer

In this viewpoint, the authors discuss the findings of the National Crime Victimization Survey, which examines responses from over 200,000 people who have been victims of non-fatal crimes in the previous year. The findings suggest that the rate of hate crime victimizations is considerably higher for LGBTQIA+ people than heterosexual and cisgender people. Additionally, hate crime attacks on LGBTQIA+ people have certain unique characteristics, such as that the attacker is often someone close to the victim and LGBTQIA+ victims of attacks are often more likely to experience physical and psychological symptoms after the attack. Andrew R. Flores is an assistant professor of government at the School of Public Affairs at American University. Ilan Meyer is the Williams Distinguished Senior Scholar for Public Policy at the Williams Institute of the University

"LGBTQ Americans Are 9 Times More Likely to Be Victimized by a Hate Crime," by Andrew Ryan Flores, Ilan Meyer, Rebecca Stotzer, The Conversation, December 21, 2022. https://theconversation.com/lgbtq-americans-are-9-times-more-likely-to-be-victimized-by-a-hate-crime-196717. Licensed under CC BY-ND 4.0 International.

of California, Los Angeles. Rebecca Stotzer is a professor of social work at the University of Hawaii.

As you read, consider the following questions:

1. How does the rate of hate crime victimizations for LGBTQIA+ people compare to the rate for cisgender and heterosexual people?
2. How is a hate crime defined in this viewpoint?
3. According to research cited in this viewpoint, what percent of violent hate crimes involve someone close to the victim when they are LGBTQIA+?

In our recent analysis of the National Crime Victimization Survey, we found that the odds of being a violent hate crime victim for LGBTQ people was nine times greater than it was for cisgender and straight people from 2017 to 2019.

There were an average annual 6.6 violent hate crime victimizations per 1,000 LGBTQ people during this three year period.

In contrast, there were 0.6 violent hate crime victimizations per 1,000 cisgender and straight people.

A hate crime is an attack or threat of an attack that's motivated by the victim's perceived race, ethnicity, sexuality, gender or religion. Or it could include someone's association with any of the previous categories, such as an anti-Muslim hate crime committed against someone who is Sikh.

The National Crime Victimization Survey is a nationally representative survey that asks over 200,000 people about non-fatal crimes that happened to them in the past year. Since 1999, it has asked victims if they suspected their victimization was motivated by certain biases, and if so, the reason for the bias. We use the National Crime Victimization Survey classification of hate crimes, which is consistent with the Bureau of Justice Statistics classification:

victimizations that involve hate language, hate symbols, or were confirmed by police to be a hate crime.

Since 2017, the National Crime Victimization Survey has been documenting sexual orientation and gender identity of respondents. This has allowed us to estimate the rate of hate crimes against LGBTQ people for the first time.

Hate Crimes Against LGBTQIA+ People Are Rising

Hate crimes have risen in the last year according to a study released by the Center for the Study of Hate and Extremism at California State University, San Bernardino. The nonpartisan research and policy institution said that in 2018, hate crimes rose 9% in major U.S. cities that they studied. And this change comes while crime overall in major cities has declined.

This latest increase is the fifth consecutive increase in hate crimes year over year in the United States. According to the study "the most common victims for hate crimes reported to police in major cities in 2018 were African Americans, Jews, and Gays, but Whites and Jews experienced the biggest percentage increase.

To combat this, 47 states as well as other U.S. territories like the Virgin Islands, D.C., and Puerto Rico all have hate crime laws. That said, of those states, less than 36 apply to LGBTQ+ people specifically. And this is important.

This year alone, 12 Black trans women have been murdered. Of this number, 10 of the women were killed with a gun.

Preliminary numbers for 2019 show increases with the partial data that is available. That said, according to the report, those increases will likely erode by the end of the year.

The report also says that "for the first time, a slight majority of hate crime victims now report to the police." In the past, victims may not have reported due to fear of rejection, and of being ignored, or even out of fear that they themselves may be questioned and in some way accosted by police. While this still continues, there have been some efforts made that have allowed victims to feel more comfortable in reporting crimes to authorities.

"Hate Crimes Against LGBTQ+ People Are the Highest in a Decade," by Mikelle Street, Out, August 1, 2019.

Physical and Psychological Repercussions

Another notable finding from our study suggested that violent hate crimes involving LGBTQ victims have unique characteristics.

Prior research has suggested that LGBTQ victims of hate crime frequently did not know the offender. In our analyses, 49% of violent hate crimes with LGBTQ victims involved an attacker who was a close friend, family member, partner or former partner.

We also found that LGBTQ victims of violent hate crimes were more likely to have physical and psychological symptoms as a result of the attack when compared with LGBTQ victims of violent crimes that were not hate crimes.

For example, LGBTQ victims of violent hate crimes were four times more likely to feel worried or anxious as a result of the incident than LGBTQ victims of non-hate violence. Despite this, we found that only about 1 in 3 LGBTQ victims of violent hate crimes sought professional help for their symptoms.

Hate Crimes Don't Just Affect the Victims

Our findings complement a series of studies relying on the National Crime Victimization Survey that showed that LGBTQ people are generally victims of crimes at higher rates than cisgender and straight people, with bisexual women having markedly higher victimization rates than lesbians, and transgender people having higher victimization rates than cisgender people.

Hate crimes do not just affect an individual—whole communities can be affected by hate. In what's known as "collective trauma," LGBTQ people often internalize the violence inflicted on other members of the community.

LGTBQ people are still recovering from the November 2022 mass shooting at Club Q, an LGBTQ bar in Colorado Springs. The accused shooter has been charged with 48 counts of hate-motivated violence.

Our findings allow us to more fully characterize the stories of LGBT victims—and the heightened danger they face across the country.

LGBTQIA+ Rights

Periodical and Internet Sources Bibliography

The following articles have been selected to supplement the diverse views presented in this chapter.

Arman Azad, "Many LGBTQ Youth Who Die by Suicide Are Bullied Before Their Death, Study Finds," CNN, May 26, 2020. https://www.cnn.com/2020/05/26/health/lgbtq-bullying-suicides.

Emily Bazelon, "The Fight Over Gender Therapy," *New York Times*, June 15, 2022. https://www.nytimes.com/2022/06/15/magazine/gender-therapy.html.

Max Bearak and Darla Cameron, "Here Are the 10 Countries Where Homosexuality May Be Punished by Death," *Washington Post*, June 16, 2016. https://www.washingtonpost.com/news/worldviews/wp/2016/06/13/here-are-the-10-countries-where-homosexuality-may-be-punished-by-death-2/.

Stephanie Berger-Columbia, "How Anti-Gay Prejudice Cuts Life Expectancy," Futurity, February 25, 2014. https://www.futurity.org/homophobia-causes-earlier-deaths/.

Dani Blum, "Why LGBTQ Adults Are More Vulnerable to Heart Disease," *New York Times*, June 29, 2022, updated July 13, 2022. https://www.nytimes.com/2022/06/29/well/live/lgbtq-heart-health.html.

Melissa Brown, "LGBTW Educator Visibility Can Be a Matter of Life and Death," PBS, June 26, 2020. https://www.pbs.org/newshour/classroom/2022/06/educator-voice-lgbtq-educator-visibility-can-be-a-matter-of-life-and-death/.

Josephine Lee, "At One Texas School, LGBTQ Teens Call Onslaught of Hostile Laws 'Matter of Life and Death,'" Salon, January 11, 2022. https://www.salon.com/2022/01/11/at-one-texas-school-lgbtq-teens-call-onslaught-of-hostile-laws-matter-of-life-and-death/.

James Martin, "Why Should the Church Reach out the LGBTQ People? Some Shocking Statistics Can Answer That," *American Magazine*, August 2, 2021. https://www.americamagazine.org/faith/2021/08/02/james-martin-lgbtq-catholics-statistics-241139.

Shabab Ahmed Mirza and Caitlin Rooney, "Discrimination Prevents LGBTQ People from Accessing Health Care," Center for American Progress, January 18, 2018. https://www.americanprogress.org/article/discrimination-prevents-lgbtq-people-accessing-health-care/.

Sara M. Moniuszko, "How Doctors' Assumptions about LGBTQ Patients Can Be Harmful to Their Health," *USA Today*, October 1, 2021. https://www.usatoday.com/story/life/health-wellness/2021/10/01/lgbtq-inclusive-healthcare-still-not-mainstream-heres-why/5904801001/.

Alvin Powell. "The Problems with LGBTQ Healthcare." *Harvard Gazette*, March 23, 2018. https://news.harvard.edu/gazette/story/2018/03/health-care-providers-need-better-understanding-of-lgbtq-patients-harvard-forum-says/.

OPPOSING VIEWPOINTS® SERIES

CHAPTER 4

Should Transgender People Be Allowed to Serve in the Military?

Chapter Preface

In recent years, the story of LGBTQIA+ people in the military has been one of gains and losses, ups and downs. These viewpoints, published between 2018 and 2021, discuss the situation as it unfolded during that period with references to matters that led up to the current state of affairs. As you will see in the viewpoints in this chapter, while the issue of LGBTQIA+ people in the armed forces has been debated for many years, gay, lesbian, and bisexual men and women have been allowed to openly serve since 2011, when the "Don't Ask, Don't Tell" policy was repealed. "Don't Ask, Don't Tell" was a policy whereby the military didn't ask service members to disclose their sexual orientation. However, LGBTQIA+ service members could be discharged for disclosing it. Being able to serve openly does not mean being free from discrimination, however. The first viewpoint here points out the struggles still faced by LGBTQIA+ service members.

Transgender people have had an even bumpier road to being allowed to serve their country through military service. People who do not identify with their sex assigned at birth (no matter at what stage of transitioning) were only allowed to enlist and serve in the armed forces as of 2021—and the controversy about this is still ongoing. Multiple viewpoints in this chapter offer contrasting opinions about allowing transgender men and women to serve in the armed forces. One viewpoint argues that the physical and emotional demands of transitioning are incompatible with the demands of serving in the military and will only weaken the military. Others argue that there is no medical basis for excluding transgender people from military service, and that it benefits the military to allow LGBTQIA+ people—including transgender people—to enlist.

VIEWPOINT 1

> "Despite the orders from above, many veterans publicly opposed the 2011 repeal of the ban on gay, lesbian and bisexual service members."

Bias Remains a Problem for LGBTQIA+ Service Members

Meghann Myers

This viewpoint was published in MilitaryTimes, *an independent news source providing information for members of the military and their families. This viewpoint covers the results of a study of lesbian, gay, bisexual, and transgender service members that considered responses from interviews conducted in 2016. Although lesbian, gay, and bisexual servicemembers could openly serve after "Don't Ask, Don't Tell" was repealed, many of the people surveyed were reluctant to disclose their sexuality because they worried about negative reactions and bias. However, feeling the need to hide their LGBTQIA+ identity often takes a toll on these servicemembers. Meghann Myers is Pentagon Bureau Chief at* MilitaryTimes.

As you read, consider the following questions:

1. What fears do Myers' sources mention having even after gay, lesbian, and bisexual people were given the right to serve openly?

"LGBT Service Members Are Allowed to Be Out and Proud, but a Fear of Repercussions Persists," by Meghann Myers, MilitaryTimes, June 15, 2020. Reprinted by permission.

| 138

2. Why do service people say they don't want to "stand out?"
3. What was the Trump administration's position on transgender service members? How was that different from the position of the Obama administration?

Half a decade after the repeal of don't ask, don't tell, most lesbian, gay, bisexual and transgender service members still felt reluctant to be open about their sexuality with their colleagues and chain of command, according to a study released in late May.

The study, published by the journal *Sexuality Research and Social Policy*, found that 59 percent of respondents did not feel comfortable being out at work, either because of career repercussions or because of the burden of being a token responsible for educating their peers.

"Taken together, LGBT service members seek a military in which disclosure will not subject them to negative career repercussions, burden them with feelings of differentness or expectations to teach others how to treat them, limit their ability to access needed resources for themselves or their family, and, ultimately, that their physical and personal integrity will not be endangered," the authors, both military and academic researchers, found.

Pentagon officials did not immediate respond to a request for comment about the study.

And despite a Monday Supreme Court decision which ruled that workplace discrimination against LBGT employees violates the Civil Rights Act of 1964, that decision does not include service members.

A Pentagon spokeswoman referred a request for comment to the Justice Department, as the ruling deals specifically with federal/civilian employment.

The study came out of interviews with 37 service members during 2016, at a time when Obama administration policy allowed transgender troops to take hormones as part of a transition, despite not allowing them to formalize a transition in the Defense Enrollment Eligibility Reporting System.

"Most participants ... noted a reluctance to disclose their LGBT identity due to the fear that they could be negatively affected, despite repeal of anti-LGBT policies," the study found. "These fears were not necessarily motivated by specific incidents, but rather a 'sixth sense' that it may not yet be safe to disclose LGBT identity in the military workplace."

Despite the orders from above, many veterans publicly opposed the 2011 repeal of the ban on gay, lesbian and bisexual service members.

And for troops who had grown up in that environment, the policy's demise did not flip a switch in terms of comfort level—theirs or their colleagues. According to the study 42 percent of respondents felt that the organizations culture had not caught up to the policy.

"That was a fear of mine when I joined the military was yeah, they are allowing LGBT, well, LGB people to come in, but are they actually accepting of it or is it just them saying it because they have to, kind of thing?" one respondent, a lesbian airman, said in her interview.

And even if colleagues were largely tolerant, a culture that promotes uniformity was in itself not welcoming.

"I definitely felt more like I was swimming against the stream," one respondent, a bisexual airman, said. "Like, in the military there's this idea that you do not want to stand out at all, like you want to blend in with the walls. You want to seem like everyone else. You want to be like interchangeable with other people. You do not want to stand out because you do not want to be a candidate for punishment or just seen as having discrepancies about you."

Indeed, despite the change in policy, some troops felt open hostility from leaders.

"The instructor was reported to use the pejorative term 'fags' during class, disclose other people's sexual minority identity to his students without their permission, and communicate that he believed sexual minorities were more promiscuous than heterosexuals," according the the study, based on a response from a gay soldier. "Classmates notably did not verbally protest the instructor's behaviors, which may have contributed to the sense that the instructor's beliefs, as opposed to the aggregate of students' beliefs, were paramount in creating class climate."

According to the study, 19 percent of LGBT troops were afraid of career consequences for being open about their identities. Though it was no longer a discharging offense, they feared bias could affect them more subtlely.

"I do not want to screw myself before I even have that opportunity [to be promoted]. I'm in a position ...where I am about to be put on a board for major and I do not want to not even have that opportunity to put myself where they can easily be like, 'Get rid of this guy; if we have to cut 55 percent of the officers up for it, he's one of the easy ones we can just find a reason to just cover [ourselves],' " said one respondent, a gay Marine. "So I want to be smart about it. You cannot be a positive role model if you are not even there, if you just get tossed out."

To navigate what one respondent compared to a mine field around and LGBT identity, service members looked for cues from their peers and leadership to help them figure out whether to disclose or not. According to the data, 32 percent of them had felt discouraged from being open, while 27 percent had seen signs that they should be.

"I had a few friends there [in training] that I got to know pretty well, but I knew a couple of them had some pretty strong religious backgrounds and I did not really feel like testing the waters at that point," one respondent, a gay soldier, said. "I did not know where I was going, who I was going to be working with next, so just kind of kept my nose, again, to the grindstone and pushed through the training."

Despite those concerns, 41 percent of respondents felt it was important to be open about their identities, either for their own wellbeing or to help others feel comfortable.

"When that Orlando attack happened, that was kind of a big deal. I'm like well, the best way to keep people from being homophobic is to have them have someone that they know and respect, who is gay," one sailor said. "So, I have decided that it would be a conscious decision where I would actually mention that stuff in class, just sort of in passing, especially at this sort of hypermasculine culture at the [Naval] Academy."

Others decided to keep their heads down and avoid rocking the boat.

"Obviously, I only told people who knew me already," another sailor, a trans man, said. "But I made it very clear to them. I was like 'I'm not trying to come out and be like a poster child for trans people' because as amazing as that would be, I have a feeling that there will be some people who are not cool with it and they might try to kill me on my way to my car or some professor might not be cool with it and she'll like flunk me or he'll flunk me and I just do not got time for drama right now. Like, let me just try to get through this next tour."

The Trans Question

In the summer of 2016, then-Defense Secretary Ash Carter announced that the Defense Department would lift its ban on transgender troops serving openly and seeking treatment while in uniform, which set into motion transition policy and training for commanders with a July 1, 2017, deadline.

Three weeks later, President Trump tweeted his intention to reverse those decisions, reinstating the ban and formally closing the door in 2019.

Though Trump administration policy bars transgender Americans from joining the military, it does not kick out those who are currently serving. As of April 2019, if they had not already begun or completed the transition to their identified gender, they have to serve according to their sex assigned at birth.

This year has seen some challenges to that policy. In May, the Navy granted a waiver to a female Navy lieutenant allowing her to remain uniform, despite being diagnosed with gender dysphoria in June 2019.

And on Monday, the Supreme Court ruled that the employers cannot discriminate against their homosexual or transgender employees.

"An employer who fires an individual for being homosexual or transgender fires that person for traits or actions it would not have questioned in members of a different sex," Justice Neil Gorsuch wrote in the decision. "Sex plays a necessary and undisguisable role in the decision, exactly what Title VII forbids."

It remains to be seen, however, whether that will extend to troops, as the issue of military readiness allows the services more leeway in deciding who is and isn't fit for the job.

The Trump administration has argued that a diagnosis of gender dysphoria, a type of anxiety that stems from a disconnect between a person's identified gender and their physical body, constitutes a disqualifying mental health disorder.

The Supreme Court in January ruled that the military's transgender ban can stay in effect while lower courts hash out lawsuits that seek to overturn it.

Judges in both California and the District of Columbia will hear challenges to the ban later this year, and the case law handed down by Monday's SCOTUS decision could work in favor of the plaintiffs.

VIEWPOINT 2

> "Drawing on gender stereotypes, the authors wrote, many men claimed women needed to shower more often or would be emotionally unstable during menstruation and therefore unreliable in their positions."

There Are Gender-Related Differences in Opinions on Gender-Neutral Bathrooms in the Military

Mike Krings

This viewpoint by Mike Krings covers a study about the views of military personnel about women in combat. But the main issue here is bathrooms—a topic that is also often a point of contention for trans people in the military and elsewhere. In this study, the researchers found that bathrooms are often used as a tool for maintaining segregation. A considerably lower percentage of the men surveyed were supportive of gender-neutral bathrooms compared to women surveyed. The researchers assert that this may be a way for men to protect an existing sexist culture after it was threatened by allowing women to engage in combat. The same could be argued for resistance to gender-neutral bathrooms as they relate to transgender people as well. Mike Krings is a public affairs officer at the University of Kansas.

"Study Finds Stark Divide Between Military Men, Women on Gender-Neutral Bathrooms, Reinforcing Discrimination," by Mike Krings, Phys.org, March 18, 2021. Reprinted by permission.

Should Transgender People Be Allowed to Serve in the Military?

As you read, consider the following questions:

1. What was the original purpose of having separate bathrooms for men and women, according to this viewpoint?
2. In the survey discussed in this viewpoint, were men or women more reluctant to share bathrooms with the opposite gender?
3. What types of misinformation did the men in this study have about women?

The introduction of gender-neutral restrooms into public and private spaces is a departure from more than a century of policies put in place to ostensibly "protect" women in business, schools and the military. New University of Kansas research shows a stark divide between men and women in the military in their attitudes about the existence of gender-neutral bathrooms and what they mean for gender-based stereotypes and discrimination.

In 2013, the Department of Defense lifted a policy banning women from combat positions. KU scholars conducted a series of surveys and focus groups with soldiers who are part of Army special forces, commonly known as Green Berets, about their thoughts on integration. The research was conducted from October 2013 to February 2014 at Fort Bragg in North Carolina and Fort Leavenworth in Kansas. Less than one-third of men said they would be open to sharing bathrooms with women, while nearly two-thirds of women said they had no objection to it. Those results came from research that didn't originally ask about bathroom policies.

"We weren't focused on bathrooms originally, but they kept coming up, more than 300 times," said Shannon Portillo, associate professor of public affairs & administration and associate dean for academic affairs at KU's Edwards Campus. "We were focused on larger questions of military integration, but we saw a stark gender difference on this topic. The results clearly showed men were concerned about continuing a sex-separated atmosphere."

Portillo co-wrote the study with Alesha Doan, professor of public affairs & administration and in the Department of Women, Gender & Sexuality Studies, and KU alumna Ashley Mog, U.S. Department of Veterans Affairs. The study was recently published in the journal *Armed Forces and Society*.

"When a male-dominated organization makes positive policy changes to reduce gender inequity, it can simultaneously trigger pushback from the rank-and-file men, who may react by attempting to 're-gender' the organization by doubling down on the existing sexist culture," said Doan, noting they found that exact dynamic in their research.

While policies such as the rescinding of a ban of women in combat positions has led to integration, results of the 27 focus groups of special forces members—many deployed to sites such as Iraq and Afghanistan—show there is still resistance and efforts to maintain gender segregation, the authors wrote.

Men frequently cited privacy, risk and hygiene as factors they felt warranted separate facilities. In terms of privacy, however, they only stated they needed privacy from women, not from other men, or to be able to use facilities by themselves. In terms of hygiene and risk, men were focused on menstruation and showed misunderstanding of and revulsion about the topic. Drawing on gender stereotypes, the authors wrote, many men claimed women needed to shower more often or would be emotionally unstable during menstruation and therefore unreliable in their positions.

Women also dispelled the assumption that more financial resources would be necessary to accommodate them as part of special forces and combat units. They dismissed the idea that they needed new bathroom or shower facilities, noting they could use stalls for both toilets and showers, cover with towels when necessary or put a sign on a door that a facility was in use. Others said unisex bathrooms were not an issue as they have used them in other areas of life.

While men commonly said they did not oppose integration of combat forces, their assumptions about bathrooms and women,

Independent Analysis Finds Cost of Transgender Soldiers Minimal

In his Wednesday morning tweet-storm announcing that transgender people would no longer be allowed to serve in the military, President Trump said the move stemmed from the "tremendous medical costs and disruption that transgender in the military would entail."

However, an analysis by the Rand Corporation last year found that the costs of allowing transgender people to serve in the military would have a "minimal impact" on the budget, amounting to $2.4 million to $8.4 million each year, or 0.04 percent to 0.13 percent of the military health care budget. That's little more than a rounding error when compared to the total U.S. military budget of roughly $700 billion.

Rand estimates that there are 2,500 transgender people currently on active duty in the military, and about 1,500 in the reserves. It estimates that 29 to 129 service members might seek transition-related care, which could leave them unable to deploy immediately.

Last month, Defense Secretary Jim Mattis ordered a six-month delay to an Obama policy that would have allowed transgender people to enlist. Conservatives largely opposed that policy. Eighteen countries currently allow transgender people to serve in their militaries.

Transgender rights have been a contentious issue in recent years as states debate so-called "bathroom bills," which require people to use the restroom that matches the gender designated on their birth certificate. The Trump administration has reversed an Obama administration policy that mandated schools allow students to use bathrooms of their choice.

"How Much Do Transgender Soldiers Really Cost the US Military?" by Beth Braverman, The Fiscal Times, July 26, 2017.

and statements about needing to protect women from risks, belied a misunderstanding about bathroom policies, how they have been used to keep women out of certain spaces and to continue gender separation and privilege they have grown accustomed to, the authors wrote.

"The men in the focus groups held on to the idea of bathrooms not being neutral. They made clear they were not trying to be sexist but did acknowledge bathroom policies that have kept women out of certain public spaces for decades," Portillo said. "Women are trying to access a space that has been exclusively male and are willing to adapt to do so. Men said they were OK with it but were not willing to open certain spaces."

The authors also shared a history of American bathroom policy, pointing out how gendered restrooms were first put in place in public in the late 19th century as more women were entering the workforce and a lack of women's restrooms had been used to justify not hiring women, among other discriminatory practices.

The study is the third part of a larger research project Doan and Portillo have undertaken about the integration of combat forces. They previously published a study on cultural aspects of a male-dominated military and a book on how "organizational obliviousness" has allowed entrenched gender stereotypes to slow integration. And while President Joe Biden recently lifted a ban on transgender individuals openly serving in the military, the studies focused only on cisgender individuals, as the ban was in place at the time of the research.

The findings illustrate how toilets were a focal point for special forces members to attempt to re-establish gender segregation in a changing military atmosphere. That reflects not only what is happening currently as policies are debated to prevent gender-neutral facilities in schools and public places, but the long history of bathrooms being used as a way of keeping women out of certain professions such as policing, Congress, firefighting and others, based on assumptions about privacy, risk and hygiene.

"This is not just something that is contained in the military. There has been a long history of bathroom politics in the workplace," Portillo said. "It's also being discussed in schools, and it all shows us just how much bathrooms are a part of public life. They have been and are being used as a way to maintain segregation."

VIEWPOINT 3

> "The facts show that thrusting individuals with gender dysphoria into a stressful military environment would have devastating consequences."

Transgender Service Members Will Weaken the Military

Thomas Spoehr

Previous viewpoints in this chapter have discussed various details about the experience of LGBTQIA+ members of the military and how gender and sexuality affect this experience, but this is the first to make an argument against allowing LGBTQIA+ Americans to serve. Here, the author argues that allowing transgender people to serve will weaken the military. Spoehr argues that transgender people experience higher rates of gender dysphoria, which is linked to higher rates of mental health issues. Additionally, he asserts that the medical procedures involved in transitioning are at odds with the physical standards for deployment. Thomas W. Spoehr is a retired Army lieutenant general and director of the Heritage Foundation's Center for National Defense.

As you read, consider the following questions:

1. What is gender dysphoria and why is the definition of this term important to the argument in this viewpoint?

"How Joe Biden's New Transgender Policy Will Weaken Our Military," by Thomas Spoehr, The Daily Wire, April 13, 2021. Reprinted by permission.

2. What changes did James Mattis make to policies about transgender service members when he was Secretary of Defense?
3. What data does the author cite to support his claims?

Joe Biden ran a campaign built on a vow to "return to norms." The latest policy announcement from the Department of Defense (DOD) calls that promise into question.

Under President Biden's new policy, individuals who identify as transgender, and have been diagnosed with gender dysphoria, will not only be allowed to serve in the U.S. military, but will have their "gender transitions" paid for by American taxpayers.

Biden's policy undoes decades of military practice, and more importantly, decades of common sense.

Facts are important here. Before 2016, U.S. military policy generally did not allow transgender individuals to enlist. In 2016, the Obama administration changed the policy to allow unrestricted military service by transgender individuals, including those with gender dysphoria.

After months of careful study, the Pentagon under Defense Secretary James Mattis modified this policy, prohibiting individuals from serving if they were suffering from gender dysphoria, or had a recent history of suffering from the condition. Everyone else who was qualified could serve.

Many on the left and in the media falsely termed this a "transgender ban," when in fact, it was anything but. It was an important step taken only after thoughtful deliberation to ensure that America's men and women in uniform were not put at risk in a rush to engage in social engineering with our armed forces.

The facts show that thrusting individuals with gender dysphoria into a stressful military environment would have devastating consequences.

The report issued by the administration in 2019 uncovered several striking findings from medical experts:

Should Transgender People Be Allowed to Serve in the Military?

- Service members with gender dysphoria are eight times more likely to attempt suicide than service members as a whole (12% versus 1.5%).
- These individuals are nine times more likely to have mental health encounters than the service member population as a whole (28.1 average encounters versus 2.7)
- Individuals with gender dysphoria experience severe anxiety—between eight and nine times the rate of individuals without gender dysphoria.

These numbers are critically important in ways that America's elites will never understand.

Military service is inherently stressful, especially so in a combat environment. Every member of the unit depends on the person next to him or her. They have trained and worked together constantly. Their relationship is one of trust—they know everyone has each other's back.

Allowing mistrust or uncertainty into the unit weakens this critical bond. It breeds resentment. It causes doubt where once was certainty.

This is the heart of the transgender service debate. If those with gender dysphoria are at a much higher risk of suicide, crippling anxiety or other mental breakdowns than their peers, those serving next to them will be reluctant to rely on them. Permitting them to serve also violates the principle of not placing individuals at greater risk of injury in harm's way.

Further, the Pentagon is creating a class of potentially non-deployable service members. The physical standards for deployments, even non-combat deployments, are rigorous and exacting, and do not allow for the intense medical requirements of "gender transition" procedures or their aftermath. This will harm readiness not just by reducing the number of available warfighters, but by breeding resentment among units who have members everyone knows will not be called upon to deploy with the rest of the unit.

Not only is the Biden administration allowing these fractures to develop, it is actively encouraging them.

This policy will weaken the U.S. military and signal to our enemies that the force is more concerned with political correctness than in challenging our adversaries and protecting our interests.

While China and Russia are busy investing in their military capabilities and seeking new ways to kill Americans and threaten our interests, the Biden administration is promising to not only welcome individuals with once-disqualifying medical conditions into the ranks, but to reward those individuals with taxpayer-funded "gender reassignment" surgeries and time off away from their unit and training regimen to recover.

But don't worry—those taxpayer dollars will only add up to "a handful of a million dollars," according to the Pentagon.

As usual, the consequences of this decision will be felt by the men and women responsible for our security, not the policymakers in DC.

VIEWPOINT 4

> "Fitness to serve is not about who we love, the color of our skin, or our gender."

Transgender Service Members Will Make the Military Stronger

Christian Fuscarino

In this viewpoint, Christian Fuscarino makes an argument for allowing LGBTQIA+ Americans to serve their country. Allowing people of color and women to serve made the military stronger. Allowing gay and lesbian people to serve made the military stronger. The same, he argues, will happen if the U.S. allows transgender people to serve. This viewpoint was originally published in 2019, when the Trump administration enacted policies that prevented many transgender people from serving in the military. Christian Fuscarino is executive director of Garden State Equality, New Jersey's largest LGBTQIA+ advocacy and education organization.

As you read, consider the following questions:

1. Why was the timing of the ban on transgender service members particularly bad, according to this viewpoint?
2. According to this viewpoint, how does the transgender ban divide the public?

"Can't We Just Let Transgender Americans Serve Their Country, a Husband Asks," by Christian Fuscarino, NJ Advance Media, April 12, 2019. Reprinted by permission. NJ Advance Media.

3. According to Fuscarino, what is special about being able to serve in the military?

My husband, Aaron, is currently serving in the United States Marine Corps. Aaron will freely tell you that he does not care who is in the trenches next to him as long as they know how to shoot a rifle, destroy the enemy, and complete the mission. The only consideration is "as the first to fight, are you fit to serve?" Fit to serve whether male or female. Fit to serve whether black, brown, or white. Fit to serve whether gay, straight or transgender.

Today, Aaron is respected and celebrated by his peers and his officers. He wakes up every morning, works hard, and trains hard. He has expert shooter marksmanship, and he's proud to be partaking in the most important public and civic duty that he's ever known: military service.

While he always dreamed of serving in the ultimate rifle club, he did not always have that opportunity. If he, or even his father, had been born a few decades earlier, they both would have been barred due to the color of their skin.

And in case you missed my byline, Aaron also happens to be gay. Until just a few years ago, able public servants like my husband—ready and willing to fight for the United States and defend our freedoms across the globe—were barred from service because they were openly gay. People like Aaron were said to be a threat to troop morale and unit cohesion.

There were concerns about the burdensome physical and psychological demands. However, since the repeal of Don't Ask, Don't Tell, we know that allowing openly gay troops has not hurt the military as opponents decried, but, in fact, has benefitted the military. When surveyed after the repeal, troops reported that morale, officer and troop quality, and overall quality of life were all better or higher.

Now, in a heartless attempt to divide the public and deny a group of citizens the opportunity to serve our country, the Trump administration has enacted a policy that would callously ban transgender Americans from the military. Beginning Friday, almost 15,000 active and reserve transgender service members are at risk of being discharged, while countless more will be denied enlistment.

The administration is now using the same old, outdated, unsupported arguments to ban transgender troops that were used against people like my husband. The same arguments used about gays, about blacks, and about women. Over the decades of gradually expanding our nation's defenses to be inclusive of women, people of color, and gays and lesbians, none of the fear-mongering has proven to be true.

This misguided and discriminatory ban could not come at a worse time. While our military fitness is stronger than ever, our recruitment is down substantially. And even though Americans have been enlisting at lower numbers, transgender Americans serve in the military at twice the rate of the general population. I am inclined to believe that is because transgender Americans—one of the most marginalized communities in our country—acutely understand the significance of our nation's freedoms and the importance of defending them at all costs.

Conversely, while transgender Americans have overwhelmingly been standing up to defend our nation, our Commander in Chief is a confessed draft dodger who jokes about how he got a doctor's note for his bone spur. Just as quickly and thoughtlessly as he rejected service to his country, he Tweeted the announcement of the ban, which sent both military leaders and his lawyers scrambling to catch up. I am not open to advice from him on who is fit to serve alongside my husband in the trenches.

Instead, the President would be wise to listen to Americans who have actually served. Over forty retired military officers joined to say Trump's policy "contradicts the actual judgment of both current and former senior military leaders, as well as medical research and the experiences of our own military..." The American Psychological Association and American Psychiatric Association agree that the administration's conclusions had no basis in science.

Opponents of inclusion did not think Aaron could serve. They did not think his father could serve. They did not think women could serve. They have been wrong every time. Fitness to serve is not about who we love, the color of our skin, or our gender. As part of the first group of Marines to serve after Don't Ask, Don't Tell was repealed, Aaron proves that every day. And more significantly, the transgender troops who have been serving openly and bravely since 2016 prove that, too.

Each of us is earning a piece of freedom for ourselves and our fellow citizens when we participate in public service, especially in the military. The opportunity to actively participate in and develop one's democracy simply does not exist in some countries. To exclude transgender service members from that opportunity is a contradiction of our values and defies everything about the spirit of America. Let transgender Americans serve.

VIEWPOINT 5

> "Transgender people have long served in the armed forces. The Williams Institute, a think tank at the University of California in Los Angeles, estimates that roughly 134,000 transgender Americans hold veteran status."

Transgender Troops Are Fit to Serve in the Military

Brandon Hill and Joshua Trey Barnett

In this viewpoint, the authors discuss research they have conducted on transgender service members and veterans and how it relates to policies imposing limits on transgender troops. They argue that these policies conflict with the medical understanding of gender dysphoria by claiming that all people who are transgender experience gender dysphoria, which medical professionals do not believe to be the case. Furthermore, the authors assert that the argument that allowing transgender people to serve in the military would have a high medical cost is false. According to this viewpoint, many transgender troops have served in the military despite limits that have been imposed since the 1960s, and it benefits the military to openly allow transgender people to serve. Brandon Hill is Executive Director of the Center for Interdisciplinary Inquiry and Innovation in Sexual and Reproductive

"Trump's Military Policy Overlooks Data on Why Transgender Troops Are Fit to Serve," by Brandon Hill and Joshua Trey Barnett, The Conversation, April 2, 2018. https://theconversation.com/trumps-military-policy-overlooks-data-on-why-transgender-troops-are-fit-to-serve-94058. Licensed under CC BY 4.0 International.

Health at the University of Chicago. Joshua Trey Barnett is a professor of rhetoric at the University of Minnesota, Duluth.

As you read, consider the following questions:

1. Did the definition of gender dysphoria used by the Trump administration in their policy limiting transgender troops align with the medical definition of gender dysphoria? If not, how did it differ?
2. When did the American Psychiatric Association stop classifying transgender people as having "gender identity disorder?"
3. According to research cited in this viewpoint from the RAND National Defense Research Institute, how would offering benefits for health care coverage for gender transition-related treatments affect the military's budget?

The Trump administration released a memorandum on March 23 that imposes limits on transgender troops and excludes transgender people from enlistment in the U.S. military.

The policy states that individuals with a history of "gender dysphoria" are now disqualified from military service "except under certain limited circumstances." It defines people with gender dysphoria as "those who may require substantial medical treatment, including through medical drugs or surgery." This is a deviation from the medical definition of gender dysphoria. The American Psychiatric Association defines it as "a conflict between a person's physical or assigned gender and the gender with which he/she/they identify."

Since 2014, we have been working with transgender service members and veterans to better understand their experiences. Our work is part of a large and growing body of scientific research President Donald Trump, and conservatives more broadly, have ignored.

The evidence is conclusive: Transgender people are fit to serve in the U.S. military.

Medical Rationale

In the U.S., transgender individuals were officially barred from serving in the armed forces starting in the 1960s. The early prohibition was based on a now-outdated psychiatric classification. Until 2013, the American Psychiatric Association classified transgender people as having "gender identity disorder." This disqualified them for military service, along with anyone else who exhibited a mental disorder.

Since the 1980s, the U.S. armed forces barred service of any person with a "current or history of psychosexual conditions including but not limited to exhibitionism, transsexualism, transvestism, voyeurism, and other paraphilia." This view conflates transgender identity with mental illness and distress. It assumes that all transgender people experience gender dysphoria. That is false.

In 2015, the American Medical Association adopted a formal policy stating that there is no medical rationale for excluding transgender people from openly serving in the military.

Serving Under a Ban

Transgender people have long served in the armed forces. The Williams Institute, a think tank at the University of California in Los Angeles, estimates that roughly 134,000 transgender Americans hold veteran status.

About 15,000 transgender people are currently serving across all branches of the U.S. armed forces, including the National Guard and Reserve forces. The vast majority have served under the transgender ban.

In our research, we have found that transgender service members have had to conceal their identities. In fact, among the transgender service members we surveyed under the transgender military ban, only 16.2 percent reported being "out" as transgender to friends within their military unit. Only 5.6 percent were out to their commanding officer. This has limited their access to support services and health care, and made it difficult to gain institutional recognition.

It is also in stark contrast to their personal lives. The majority of those surveyed reported being out to immediate family members (72.2 percent) and nonmilitary friends (69.4 percent).

Our findings suggest that transgender individuals enlist for many of the same reasons as cisgender men and women, those whose assigned sex at birth corresponds with their gender identity. Transgender people are motivated by educational goals, career aspirations, travel, family history, patriotism and stability. Transgender service members also report few mental or physical health issues that would limit them from meeting fitness criteria.

Research conducted by the nonprofit RAND National Defense Research Institute has found similar evidence. RAND was commissioned by the government to conduct a wide-ranging external study to assess the impact of transgender service.

RAND reported that extending health care coverage for gender transition–related treatments would create only small increases in the budgets for the Department of Defense and Homeland Security. It estimated increases between US$2.4 million to $8.4 million, which represented only 0.04 to 0.13 percent of the departments' budgets. That is in direct contrast to President Trump's statement in July 2017 that it would incur "tremendous medical costs." The report also noted that transgender service has minimal impact on unit readiness and cohesion. It recommended that military fitness policies align with contemporary medical standards.

Impact of a Military Ban

President Trump's memorandum referenced inaccurate information. It undermines several rigorous scientific studies, peer-reviewed publications, the expert opinions of military leaders and officers, and the medical recommendations of our nation's leading professional organizations.

Most concerning, however, in our opinion, is that the current commander-in-chief discredits the service and sacrifices of tens of thousands of transgender veterans and service members. They have served and will continue to proudly serve our country despite persistent injustice and inequality.

LGBTQIA+ Rights

Periodical and Internet Sources Bibliography

The following articles have been selected to supplement the diverse views presented in this chapter.

Ross Benes, "How Exclusion from the Military Strengthened Gay Identity in America," *Rolling Stone*, October 3, 2016. https://www.rollingstone.com/culture/culture-news/how-exclusion-from-the-military-strengthened-gay-identity-in-america-125267/.

Thomas Brading, "Army's First Openly Gay General Retires after Inspiring Others," U.S. Army News Service, June 1, 2021. https://www.army.mil/article/247068/armys_first_openly_gay_general_retires_after_inspiring_others.

Casey Chalk, "What Is the New 'Woke' Military Really Preparing Us For?" *American Conservative*, November 8, 2019. https://www.theamericanconservative.com/what-is-the-woke-military-really-preparing-us-for/.

Nekko L. Fanning, "I Thought I Could Serve as an Openly Gay Man in the Army. Then Came the Death Threats," *New York Times*, April 10, 2019. https://www.nytimes.com/2019/04/10/magazine/lgbt-military-army.html.

Philip Klein, "The Trans-Movement Is Failing Where the Gay Rights Movement Succeeded," *American Conservative*, March 10, 2022. https://www.nationalreview.com/2022/03/the-trans-movement-is-failing-where-the-gay-rights-movement-succeeded/.

Dan Lamothe, "Trump Wants to Ban Transgender Military Troops, His Top General Feels Differently," *Washington Post*, September 26, 2017. https://www.washingtonpost.com/news/checkpoint/wp/2017/09/26/trump-wants-to-ban-transgender-military-troops-his-top-general-feels-differently/.

Lindsay Mahowald, "LGBTQ Military Members and Veterans Face Economic House and Health Insecurities," Center for American Progress, April 28, 2022. https://www.americanprogress.org/article/lgbtq-military-members-and-veterans-face-economic-housing-and-health-insecurities/.

Shirleene Robinson, "I Didn't Know that Life Existed: How Lesbian Women Found a Life in the Armed Forces," the *Conversation*, January 28, 2018. https://theconversation.com/i-didnt-know-that-world-existed-how-lesbian-women-found-a-life-in-the-armed-forces-88943.

U.S. Department of Defense, "LGBTQ in the Military: A Brief History, Current Policies and Safety," Military One Source, March 19, 2021. https://www.militaryonesource.mil/military-life-cycle/friends-extended-family/lgbtq-in-the-military/

Laurel Wamsley, "Pentagon Releases New Policies Enabling Transgender People to Serve in the Military," NPR, March 31, 2021. https://www.npr.org/2021/03/31/983118029/pentagon-releases-new-policies-enabling-transgender-people-to-serve-in-the-milit.

For Further Discussion

Chapter 1

1. In the viewpoint by Wyatt Ronan, the author points out that a large majority of Americans (including majorities of Republicans) oppose LGBTQIA+ discrimination. Why do these laws keep getting passed?
2. In addition to supporting LGBTQIA+ rights, Americans are willing to elect LGBTQIA+ candidates to office, according to data cited in the viewpoint from the *Los Angeles Blade*. However, LGBTQIA+ Americans are still underrepresented in government. Given that most people, whether they are LGBTQIA+ or not, support LGBTQIA+ rights, how important is equitable representation?
3. Acceptance of LGBTQIA+ people varies widely from country to country. The viewpoint by Jacob Poushter and Nicholas Kent in this chapter looked at some of the reasons for this. At the time of publication, the U.S. was seeing a resurgence in anti-LGBTQIA+ legislation, though it was previously a leader in LGBTQIA+ rights. What do you think accounts for that? Do the examples in this viewpoint from other countries offer any insight to that question?

Chapter 2

1. While on average men are larger and stronger than women, some women are larger and stronger than some men. Or as Katharina Lindner puts it in one viewpoint in this chapter, "the physical differences among men and among women are bigger than the differences between men and women." Given this fact, do you think that there might be other ways to group sports competitions, other than by gender? Can you think of a way to resolve the issue of trans people participating in sports that would be fair to all parties?

For Further Discussion

2. Several of the viewpoints in this chapter mention Title IX, the federal civil rights law that prohibits sex-based discrimination in school programs, including athletics, that receive federal funding. How might the issue of trans women's right to compete conflict with Title IX's ban on sex discrimination in athletics? Do you think these are valid concerns?
3. In this chapter, Katharina Lindner cited roller derby as a sport that has done a good job of handling the issue of gender. What has roller derby done differently? Do you think other sports could move away from gender segregation? Why or why not?

Chapter 3

1. How are the difficulties LGBTQIA+ people have with the health care system similar to those of straight and cisgender people? How are they different?
2. According to what you've read in the viewpoints in this chapter, what are some variables in health care that have negative health impacts for LGBTQIA+ people? What are some things that can be done to address these issues?
3. Based on what you read in the viewpoint by Andrew Ryan Flores, Ilan Meyer, and Rebecca Stotzer, what are some of the causes of hate crimes towards LGBTQIA+ people? What kinds of policies or laws could help address this issue?

Chapter 4

1. Attitudes about LGBTQIA+ people are changing quickly, as the public becomes more accepting of them. However, as you can see in this chapter on the military, policies are more complex. Why might it be difficult for LGBTQIA+ servicemembers when one administration enacts a policy about them, then the next one reverses it?
2. The viewpoint by Mike Krings in this chapter discussed a study that found men were badly misinformed about

women's issues, such as menstruation, leading to difficulties incorporating women into combat roles. Do you think similar misinformation creates problems for LGBTQIA+ people in the military? If so, how?
3. What do the authors in this chapter say about the medical rationale behind the Trump administration's limitations on transgender people serving in the military? Whose argument do you find most convincing?

Organizations to Contact

The editors have compiled the following list of organizations concerned with the issues debated in this book. The descriptions are derived from materials provided by the organizations. All have publications or information available for interested readers. The list was compiled on the date of publication of the present volume; the information provided here may change. Be aware that many organizations take several weeks or longer to respond to inquiries, so allow as much time as possible.

American Civil Liberties Union (ACLU)
125 Broad Street, 18th Floor
New York, NY 10001
(212) 549-2500
website: www.aclu.org

The ACLU was founded in 1920 to defend and protect the individual rights and liberties that are guaranteed by the Constitution of the United States. The ACLU focuses on issues including protecting the legal rights of LGBTQIA+ youth and preserving transgender rights.

Gay Lesbian and Straight Education Network (GSLEN)
110 William Street, 30th Floor
New York, NY 10038
(212) 727-0135
email: Info@glsen.org
website: www.glsen.org

GLSEN is an organization dedicated to making sure that every student in every school, no matter what sexual orientation, gender identity, or gender expression, is valued and respected. Their website includes research, resources, and information for finding a chapter near you.

Gay Straight Alliance Network (GSA)

1611 Telegraph Ave., Suite 1002
Oakland, CA 94612
(415) 552-4229
email: Info@gsanetwork.org
website: https://gsanetwork.org

A national network of gay straight alliance groups, the GSA network empowers and trains LGBTQIA+ youth to create safer schools and healthier communities. Its website includes resources on starting and operating a gay straight alliance.

GLMA: Health Professionals Advancing LGBTQ Equality

1629 K Street NW
Washington, DC 20036
(202) 478-1500
email: Info@glma.org
website: www.glma.org

Previously known as the Gay & Lesbian Medical Association, GLMA is an organization of health professionals advancing LGBTQIA+ equality. It is committed to ensuring health equity for LGBTQIA+ and all sexual and gender minority (SGM) individuals as well as equality for LGBTQIA+ and SGM health professionals in their work and learning environments.

Global Action for Trans Equality (GATE)

580 Fifth Ave, Suite 820
New York, NY 10036
email: Info@gate.ngo
website: https://gate.ngo

GATE is an advocacy organization that campaigns internationally for trans, gender diverse, and intersex rights. It works closely with UN bodies to provides resources, knowledge, and access to information on issues related to gender identity.

Human Rights Campaign (HRC)
1640 Rhode Island Ave., NW
Washington, DC 20036
(202) 628-4160
email: feedback@hrc.org
website: www.hrc.org

HRC is a leading organization in the fight for LGBTQIA+ rights. It is dedicated to ensuring that all LGBTQIA+ people, especially LGBTQIA+ people of color and trans people, are guaranteed the rights of all citizens.

Lambda Legal
120 Wall Street, 19th Floor
New York, NY 10005
(212) 809-8585
email: members@lambdalegal.org
website: www.lambdalegal.org

Lambda Legal was founded in 1973. It is the oldest and largest national legal organization dedicated to the civil rights of LGBTQIA+ people. The organization works through litigation, education, and public policy.

Learning for Justice
400 Washington Ave.
Montgomery, AL 36104
(888) 414-7752
website: www.learningforjustice.org

A project of the Southern Poverty Law Center, Learning for Justice is a group dedicated to combatting prejudice among youth and promoting equality, inclusiveness, and equitable learning environments in the classroom. One of the areas it focuses on is gender and sexual identity, and its website includes educational resources on this topic.

National LGBTQ Task Force

1050 Connecticut Ave, NW, Suite 65500
Washington, DC 20035
(202) 393-5177
website: www.thetaskforce.org

The National LGBTQ Task Force works for full freedom, justice, and equality for LGBTQIA+ people. It focuses on securing rights to equality in healthcare, housing, employment, and basic human rights.

Bibliography of Books

Samantha Allen. *Real Queer America: LGBT Stories from Red States*. New York, NY: Back Bay, 2019.

Eric Cervini. *The Deviant's War. The Homosexual versus the United States of America*. New York, NY: Picador, 2020.

Juno Dawson. *This Book Is Gay*. Naperville, IL: Sourcebooks, 2018.

Ava Lorelei Deakin. *Tomorrow Begins Now: Teen Heroes Who Faced Down Injustice*. Potomac, MD: New Degree Press, 2022.

Jeannie Gainsburg. *The Savvy Ally: A Guide for Becoming a Skilled LGBTQ+ Advocate*. Lanham, MD: Rowman and Littlefield, 2020.

Susan Gluck Mezey. *Beyond Marriage: Continuing Battles for LGBT Rights*. Lanham, MD: Rowman and Littlefield, 2017.

Florent Manelli. *50 LGBTQI+ Who Changed the World*. New Delhi, India: Supernova, 2023.

Sarah McBride. *Tomorrow Will Be Different: Love, Loss, and the Fight for Trans Equality*. New York, NY: Three Rivers Press, 2018.

Simon Napier Bell. *50 Years Legal: Welcome to Our Liberation*. Cornwall, UK: Red Planet Books, 2019.

New York Public Library, ed. *The Stonewall Reader*. New York, NY: Penguin, 2019.

Eric Rosswood and Kathleen Archambeau. *We Make it Better: The LGBTQ Community and Their Positive Contributions to Society*. Coral Gables, FL: Mango Publishing, 2019.

Ken Setterington. *Branded by the Pink Triangle*. Toronto, ON: Second Story Press, 2013.

Marc Stein. *Rethinking the Gay and Lesbian Movement.* 2nd ed. New York, NY: Routledge, 2022.

Susan Stryker. *Transgender History: The Roots of Today's Revolution.* New York, NY: Seal Press, 2017.

Tea Uglow. *Loud and Proud: Speeches that Empower and Inspire.* London, UK: White Lion, 2020.

Frank Wynne, ed. *Queer: A Collection of LGBTQ Writing from Ancient Times to Yesterday.* Chicago, IL: Head of Zeus, 2021.

Index

A

abortion, 57–58
acceptance, 25–32
adoption, 39–44, 50
Angelo, Paul J., 45–52
asexual, 14
Aston, Megan, 125–129
asylum, 48, 51

B

Barnett, Joshua Trey, 157–161
Biden, Joe, 46, 51–53, 56, 148, 150, 152
bisexual, 14, 36–37, 104, 115–116, 133, 137–138, 140
Bocci, Dominic, 45–52
Bush, George W., 56
Buttigieg, Pete, 52

C

charity, 104–106
Chulani, Vinny, 63–69
cisgender, 16, 34–35, 62, 67, 70, 72–73, 98–99, 115–117, 120, 127, 130–131, 133, 148, 160
Clinton, Bill, 56
Clinton, Hillary, 47
Congress (U.S.), 18, 36, 52, 54–58, 76
Constitution (U.S.), 15
  First Amendment, 40–43

conversion therapy, 51, 57, 105, 120
courts, 56, 76, *See also* Supreme Court
Crall, Cary S., 107–113
criminalization, 47
criminal justice system, 62

D

death penalty, 47
democracy, 36
demographics, 34
denial of service, 39–44, 48
"Don't Ask, Don't Tell," 15, 49, 137–139, 154, 156

E

economy, 24–27, 28
education, 29, 48, 76, 90, 101
elections, 33–38, 56
employment, 48–49, 51, 62, 110
European Union, 48
executive order, 46

F

Fish, Jessica N., 98–102
Flores, Andrew Ryan, 130–133
foreign policy, 18, 46, 49–52
Fuscarino, Christian, 153–156

173

G

gay, 14, 51–52, 56, 104, 115–116, 137–138, 140, 153–155
gender-affirming care, 79–80, 84–86, 107–113, 122, 152
gender dysphoria, 112, 143, 149–151, 157–159
gender expression, 100
genderqueer/diverse, 86, 100–101
Generation Z, 36

H

Harris, Kamala, 52
hate crime, 16, 21, 47–49, 97, 130–133
health care, 16, 46, 48
  COVID-19, 103–106, 128
  HIV/AIDS, 49–50, 129
  insurance, 97, 102, 110
  provider, 97, 100–102, 107–113, 125–129
  See also under transgender
Hill, Brandon, 157–161
Hogshead-Makar, Nancy, 74–82
hormones, 62, 64, 67–68, 70, 72–74, 77–80, 83–86, 91–92, 102, 108–113, 122, 139
housing, 51–52, 57, 62, 100, 104, 118
Human Rights Campaign, 19–24

I

inclusion, 14–15
intersectionality, 115–116
intersex, 14, 64, 86

Islamic State, 47

J

Jackson, Rachel, K., 107–113
Joy, Phillip, 125–129

K

Kent, Nicholas, 25–32
Krings, Mike, 144–148

L

legislation, 18, 28, 68
  Civil Rights Act of 1964, 139
  Defense of Marriage Act, 54, 56
  Equality Act, 52
  protection of rights, 45–52, 57, 100, 102
  Respect for Marriage Act, 53–54
  setbacks, 19–24, 46, 50
  states, 19–24, 69, 80, 88–89
lesbian, 14, 34, 36, 51, 56, 115–116, 133, 137–138, 140, 153, 155
Levine, Rachel, 52
Lindberg, Tim, 53–58
Lindner, Katharina, 83–86
Los Angeles Blade, 33–38

M

Marietta, Morgan, 39–44
marriage, 15, 18, 26, 28, 43, 46, 48, 50–51, 53–58
mental health, 65–67, 87, 89–90, 98–112, 114–124, 130, 133, 143, 149, 151, 155, 158–160

Index

Meyer, Ilan, 130–133
military, 15–16, 18, 46, 48, 136–161, *See also under* transgender
Mills, Evan, 70–73
Minority Stress Model, 118
Myers, Meghann, 138–143

N

National Collegiate Athletic Association (NCAA), 24, 70–73, 75–79, 81
Native American, 37
nonbinary, 22, 35, 86, 115–117, 119–122

O

Obama, Barack, 46, 49–51, 53, 56–57, 139, 147, 150
Olympics, 62, 68, 73–81, 84–86

P

politics, 25–28, 30–31
Pope Francis, 51
Poushter, Jacob, 25–32
pride, 15
puberty, 62, 68, 71–72, 74–76, 78, 102, 111–112

Q

queer, 35, 115

R

race/ethnicity, 35, 111, 114–117, 132, 153–156

refugee, 50
religion, 21–22, 25–27, 31–32, 39–44, 48, 50–51, 105
Ronan, Wyatt, 19–24

S

safety, 97, 104, 116, 118–119, 127, 130–133
Sanders, 63–69
school, 20–21, 35, 100–101, 118–119, 121, 147
Spoehr, Thomas, 149–152
Stander, Willem, 103–106
Stonewall, 15
Stotzer, Rebecca, 130–133
substance use/abuse, 98–100
suicide, 65, 79, 97, 99–100, 114–124, 151
Supreme Court, 56, 139, 143
  Dobbs v. Jackson Women's Health Organization, 57–58
  Fulton v. Philadelphia, 39–44
  Obergefell v. Hodges, 15, 18, 43, 50, 57–58
Surprenant, Chris W., 87–93

T

Thomas, Andrew, 125–129
Thomas, Lia, 70–79, 82
Title IX, 71, 73, 75–76, 81, 88, 90
Toonen v. Australia, 47
transgender, 14
  bathroom 22, 24, 144–148
  birth certificate, 21, 64–65, 121

LGBTQIA+ Rights

health care, 20–23, 49–50, 62, 100–102, 107–113, 147, 149, 151, 157–158, 160

leaders, 34, 36, 52

military, 50–51, 137–140, 142–143, 148–156

sports, 16, 20–24, 62–95

transition, 77–78, 80, 108–113, 137, 139–140, 142, 147, 149–152, 158, 160

violence against, 48, 133

youth, 15, 20–24, 35, 64–69, 76, 79, 87–90, 108, 111, 115–117, 119–122

Trevor Project, 114–124

Trump, Donald, 18, 23, 46, 50, 53, 55, 57, 139, 142–143, 147, 153–154, 158, 160

U

United Nations, 47, 50–51

Y

Yogyakarta Principles, 47

youth, 57, 90–91, 97–102, 114–124, *See also under* transgender